Lost Children

Ulverston Workhouse in the 19th Century

J.Whitehead

Published by
HANDSTAND PRESS
48 Market Street
Ulverston
CUMBRIA LA12 7LS
Tel: 01229 588858
Email:bookshop@thetinnersrabbit.co.uk
www.ulverstonbookshops.co.uk

ISBN 095520092X

Produced by Reminder Press
Printed by Calderprint Ltd
Cover design by Martin Copley

Cover photograph by kind permission of the National Children's Homes.

the children's charity

This book has been published with financial assistance from Kirby Archive Trust

CONTENTS

LIST OF ILLUSTRATIONS

ACKNOWLEDGEMENTS

The research on which this book is based was carried out as part of the Department of Continuing Education Local History Course at Lancaster University; therefore thanks are due to Dr. Hilary Walklett and Dr. Mike Winstanley of Lancaster University History Department for their tuition and guidance. I would also like to thank Mr. Aidan Jones, District Archivist at Barrow Record Office, for his help and encouragement; Bernard and Liz Ellis, who willingly shared their wide knowledge of Ulverston workhouse history and photographs; Sister Diana Hatton and Nurse Mary Smith, ex-Ulverston N.H.S. Hospital, who kindly showed me round those parts of the hospital which were once the workhouse; Ms Alison Hardingham, Dietitian at Furness General Hospital, for taking the trouble to make a detailed analysis of the workhouse diet; Furness Family History Society for kindly allowing me to reproduce their map of the ancient parishes of Furness; Jack Layfield, Daniel Birtwistle and Ulverston Heritage Centre (now 'Heritage First'). For use of their photographs, I am grateful to: Jennifer Snell, J. Garbutt, Harry Wilson and Brian Lancaster, also to Steven White of Carlisle Library for help in obtaining permission to include the photograph of Ulverston circa 1860; likewise, Jackie Fay of Kendal Local Studies Library for photograph of Stott Park Bobbin Mill and Barrow Record Office for the diagram of the workhouse taken from the 1852 map also the photograph of 'Boy Collecting Bobbins' from the North Lonsdale Magazine Vol.III. The cover photograph is by kind courtesy of the National Children's Homes. Last, but not least, I would especially like to thank, Liz Drew, whose enthusiastic support of local history has made this publication possible.

The information used is taken primarily from the Ulverston Union Records still available – the interpretation is my own. It has never been my intention to cause distress to any living relative of those featured; in my opinion, no one should be stigmatised because of poverty or circumstance of birth.

FOREWORD

We have many things to be proud of in our history, but the Victorian workhouse system is not one of them. Despite many high-sounding ideals by those commissioned to produce it, the system evolved into something feared by all of the poor and needy.

It is now hard to believe that in a period of great industrial growth and prosperity for this country there was also such desperate poverty, especially in the cities, and that those in greatest need were treated with so little sensitivity. The workhouses were grim, dispassionate institutions, often overcrowded and badly run and the stigma associated with them persisted long after many of the buildings were taken over and used as hospitals. No amount of new paint could eliminate it from the minds of the older generations and many sad stories were told to those nursing in Ulverston Hospital during the years when its days as a workhouse were still in living memory. This sad time in our history now lives on only in the novels of Dickens or in tales handed down through the generations.

The Ulverston Hospital building in Stanley Street was originally the workhouse for the whole of the Furness area. With the demolition of this building, its place in Ulverston's history and that of the many thousands of souls who lived, and sometimes died, within its walls is in danger of being forgotten.

As industrialisation reached into Furness and in particular the iron ore industry grew to immense proportions, itinerant workers came to the area seeking work. When work or health failed, they and their families could find themselves entering the workhouse to survive. Men travelled from place to place looking for work and could find a bed for the night in the vagrant wards. To pay for their night's lodging they would be made to work, usually breaking stones, before going on their way. As we travel along the modern road from Ulverston towards Arrad Foot, we should spare a thought for those men who broke the stones which were used to build the original road, at one shilling a yard in 1862. The inmates swept the streets, women worked in the laundry, the kitchens, cleaning and scrubbing. The house was as near self-sufficient as was possible. However, the pigs that were kept in the sties behind the main buildings never provided meat for the inmates' table – they were sold at market and the money went to the workhouse treasurer. The vegetables, grown mostly by the boys, were likewise sold at market.

When I started my research into the Ulverston Poor Law Union, it soon became clear that children formed a large proportion of the workhouse population at every census throughout the period covered. I decided to try to discover who they were, why they were in the workhouse, what their life was like inside and what had happened to them after they left. Many of these children were orphans and perhaps it can be argued that life was better for them in this institution than it would have been outside. We will never know. Following them through the records, they became real people and I felt strongly that their story should be told. There are, perhaps, many families in Ulverston and the surrounding areas who are descendants of these children. I hope they will find this small history of interest and perhaps of help in tracing their ancestors. I hope, also, that they will agree with me that the workhouse children should be remembered, that their memory should not be swept away, as that ugly, but historically important, building was in 2004.

The period covered by my research coincides almost exactly to Queen Victoria's time on the throne, the Victorian era, when family life was held to be paramount and the Queen's large family of well nurtured children was held up as the ideal model.

Fig 1-STANLEY STREET HOSPITAL - shortly before demolition in 2004

CHAPTER 1   THE NEW POOR LAW

By the beginning of the 19th century, the costs of caring for the poor had escalated, particularly in the industrialised towns, and there was growing dissatisfaction amongst those forced to pay the ever-increasing poor rates. In 1832, therefore, a Royal Commission was set up to find a solution to the problem. The result was the 1834 Poor Law Amendment Act. This Act took away the power of the parishes and overseers and decreed that "all relief whatever to able-bodied persons or their families, otherwise than in well regulated workhouses...shall be declared unlawful and shall cease". The Commissioners hoped that by enforcing entry into the workhouse in order to obtain poor relief, the able-bodied would be deterred from applying and costs would therefore be reduced. It also meant that the distribution of relief would be more uniform throughout the country.

Prior to the Act of 1834, and since Elizabethan times, poor relief was the responsibility of each local parish, with local landowners, businessmen, farmers or clergy serving as parish vestrymen, responsible for collecting in the poor rates and distributing them to those most in need, but only if they had a legal settlement in the parish based on birth or length of residence. The vestry met fortnightly in the church, or vestry, and parishioners were required to appear in person to ask for help in bad times of poor harvests when work was hard to come by or when unable to work due to illness. Depending upon eligibility and circumstances, small amounts were given towards house rent, food, clothes or fuel, and apprenticeships arranged for the children once they reached the age of nine years, usually to local farmers or tradesmen, many of whom served as vestrymen. However, in urban parishes where there were many children and little or no employment, they were sent wherever a place could be found, no matter how far from home. Parents who objected to their child or children being apprenticed could be refused parish relief. The parish-based system gave relief in times of need and though inevitably prone to prejudice or favouritism, it was generally administered with some compassion. After the 1834 Act, however, groups of parishes and townships were joined together to form "Unions" with each union having one central workhouse for the surrounding area and all those deemed "able-bodied" (including orphans, unmarried mothers and their children) must enter the workhouse in order to claim relief. The old who had no family to care for them were also admitted. Overseen by the Poor Law Commissioners in London and enforced by local boards of guardians, it became known as the "workhouse system".

In compliance with the Act, the Ulverston Poor Law Union was formed on 12th August 1836; it covered all of the townships and parishes of Lonsdale North-of-the-Sands (Figs 2 and 3) The area covered was predominantly rural and agriculture was still the main industry, though slate quarrying and iron ore mining were soon to overtake it.

1

Fig 2 - TOWNSHIPS COMPRISING ULVERSTON UNION

Covering all the parishes and townships of Lonsdale North of the Sands

Population:	1841	1851	1861	1871	1881
Aldingham	907	968	1011	1061	1152
Allithwaite Lower	807	888	932	1009	975
Allithwaite Upper	740	746	729	776	713
Angerton	36	32	31	36	32
Barrow-in-Furness				18911	47259
Blawith	173	229	193	146	158
Broughton East	458	470	534	1007	1251
Broughton West	1250	1297	1183	1085	1171
Cartmel Fell	356	351	308	297	293
Church Coniston	1148	1287	1324	1106	965
Claife	541	540	540	563	547
Colton	1983	2008	1794	1860	1783
Dalton-in-Furness	3231	4683	9152	8983*	13339
Dunnerdale & Seathwaite	354	321	289	291	299
Egton-with-Newland	1024	1222	1231	1148	998
Hawkshead with Monk Coniston					
with Skelwith	1362	1271	1444	1085	1205
Holker Lower	1070	1225	1160	1115	1093
Holker Upper	1114	1134	1035	850	849
Kirkby Ireleth	1809	1728	1666	1763	1722
Lowick	374	411	468	463	376
Mansriggs	63	64	69	73	64
Osmotherley	298	225	419	405	474
Pennington	388	489	879	1112	1698
Satterthwaite	420	472	397	394	452
Staveley- in- Cartmel	1382	399	409	438	426
Subberthwaite	147	150	152	146	149
Torver	199	193	194	209	202
Ulverston	5352	6742	7414	7607	10008
Urswick	761	891	1080	1144	1287

*Barrow shown separately from Dalton
(Ref: Dalton-in-Furness District Local Board Abstract of Accounts year ending 25/03/1887- Barrow Record Office)

In 1836, the town of Ulverston was a reasonably affluent and bustling place, with many trades and small industries, farms, tanneries and mills within its boundaries. It also had a thriving shipping trade. The town was a centre for social activities in the area and boasted bowling greens, theatres, bookshops and assembly rooms for concerts, dramas and lectures. Wealthy farmers took houses in the town so that their wives and daughters could enjoy the social scene. This meant an increase in the businesses of those who served them – grocers, drapers, shoemakers, clockmakers, wine merchants, etc.

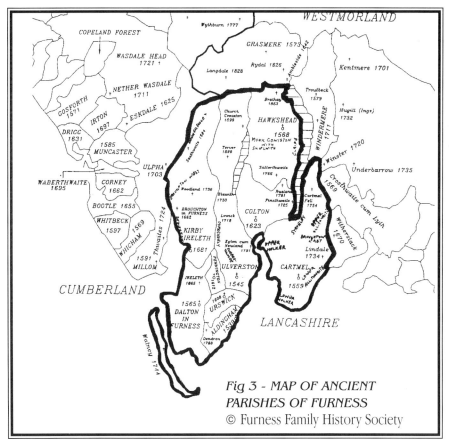

*Fig 3 - MAP OF ANCIENT
PARISHES OF FURNESS*
© Furness Family History Society

However, there was poverty both in the town and in the surrounding areas with 1,582 paupers in Furness and Cartmel in 1836 and housing was often poor, unsanitary and overcrowded. Most of the farms were small-scale, the slate quarries were not always profitable and quarrymen were constantly in danger from accident, and the once flourishing cotton mills were reducing in numbers. Thus, loss of work through accident, illness, poor weather or closure of businesses meant hardship.

The Ulverston Union Workhouse was built in Stanley Street in 1837-1838. It conformed to the standard cruciform design approved by the Commissioners (see Fig 4). The Board of Guardians charged with its management consisted of landowners, businessmen and clergy, representing the various parts of the district covered. The Earl of Burlington (later 7th Duke of Devonshire) was appointed Chairman, a position he would hold for more than fifty years.

In December 1838 the first inmates arrived from the old Colton Workhouse and Ulverston's Neville Street Workhouse, followed in January 1839 by those from Dalton and surrounding districts. By the time of the first census in 1841, children represented almost 45% of inmates and many were orphans; in the words of the historian, M.A.Crowther, "The only group of inmates blameless for their predicament" .

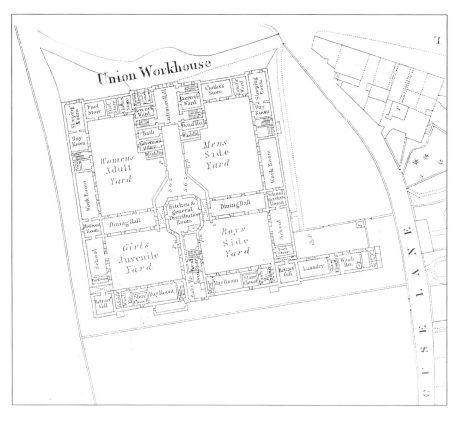

Fig 4 - DIAGRAM OF THE ULVERSTON WORKHOUSE
Detail from map of 1852

On admittance to the workhouse, all paupers were first placed in a probationary ward until examined by the medical officer to determine whether any were suffering from disease of body or mind. They were then all "thoroughly cleansed" and issued with workhouse clothes. Men and boys had their heads shaved. The clothes that each pauper wore on admittance were "purified" and kept in stores, to be returned to them on leaving the workhouse (in the case of a death, relatives would claim the clothes).

All inmates were then segregated – husbands from wives, parents from children and sister from brother. Mothers were allowed to keep their infant children with them only until they were weaned and afterwards the regulations permitted access to them "at all reasonable times". With that one exception, no pauper of one class was allowed to enter the wards or yards of any other class. It follows, therefore, that a husband would have no contact with his wife, nor a father with his daughters, nor brother with sister whilst in the workhouse system. This "Classification of Paupers" (Fig.5) was laid down by the Poor Law Commissioners. It was designed for practical administration purposes and as a further deterrent to entry. It must have been the hardest thing for most families to bear and, "In a society supposed to value the family as the school of social morality, it was the first casualty of misfortune". (*Simon Schama - A History of Britain*)

Fig 5 - CLASSIFICATION OF PAUPERS

CLASSIFICATION OF PAUPERS

1. Men and youths above seven years of age.

2. Aged and infirm women, and girls above seven years of age and under sixteen

3. Able-bodied women, and girls above sixteen.

4. Children under seven years of age.

To each class shall be assigned by the Board of Guardians that apartment or separate building which may be best fitted for the reception of such class, and which they shall respectively remain, without communication with any other class, unless as is hereinafter provided.

(Extracted from the Poor Law Commissioners' Regulations for Ulverston Union 14th December 1838 - Ref: Z1674 Furness Collection, Barrow Record Office)

The inmates were then allotted to their respective wards and so began their stay, however long, or short, in an institution dedicated to a regime of strict routine and discipline, rules and regulations (Fig 6). It would have been in marked contrast to life in a village and no-one's idea of home.

A visiting committee was appointed to inspect the house at least once a week and report back to the guardians on ventilation, cleanliness, health, work, children's schooling, performance of divine service, conduct, diet, regularity of meal times, examination of stores and enforcement of separation of classes at all times. The regulations listed twenty-three duties to be carried out by the master. These were

Fig 6 - WORKHOUSE REGULATIONS

often ex-army men, expected to be ideal for maintaining discipline, but they would lose their position if found to be violent, or if they deprived the paupers. In the early days, they had no holidays and no pension . The master's wife sometimes took the post of matron.

The matron's duties were mainly concerned with the welfare and supervision of the women and children: to see that they were clean and decent in their dress; to pay particular attention to their moral conduct and orderly behaviour and to train them in "such employments as will best fit them for service". Each night she had to ensure that they were in bed at the correct time and that all lights and fires were

the workhouse, in a case of sudden and urgent necessity, the admission of such pauper shall be brought before the Board of Guardians at their next weekly meeting, who shall decide on the propriety of the pauper's continuing in the workhouse or otherwise, and order accordingly.

IV. As soon as a pauper is admitted, he or she shall be placed in the probationary ward, or in some room to be exclusively appropriated for the purpose, and shall there remain until examined by the medical officer of the workhouse.

V. If the medical officer upon such examination pronounces the pauper to be labouring under any disease of body or mind, the pauper shall be placed either in the sick ward, or the ward for lunatics and idiots not dangerous, as the medical officer shall direct.

VI. If the medical officer pronounces the pauper to be free from disease, the pauper shall be placed in that part of the workhouse assigned to the class to which he or she may belong, and shall thereafter be treated according to the regulations hereinafter contained.

VII. Before removal from the probationary ward, the pauper shall be thoroughly cleansed, and shall be clothed in the workhouse dress, and the clothes which he or she wore upon admission shall be purified, and deposited in a place to be appropriated for that purpose, to be restored to the pauper on leaving the workhouse, or else to be used by the pauper as the Board of Guardians shall direct.

VIII. The clothing of the paupers shall be made of such materials as the Board of Guardians may determine, and shall, as far as may be practicable, be made by the paupers in the workhouse.

CLASSIFICATION OF PAUPERS.

IX. The in-door paupers, so far as the workhouse admits thereof, shall be classed as follows:—

1. Men, and youths above seven years of age.
2. Aged and infirm women, and girls above seven years of age and under sixteen.
3. Able-bodied women, and girls above sixteen.
4. Children under seven years of age.

X. To each class shall be assigned by the Board of Guardians that apartment or separate building which may be best fitted for the reception of such class, and in which they shall respectively remain, without communication with any other class, unless as is hereinafter provided.

XI. Provided,

Firstly. If the workhouse shall not be of such capacity and arrangement as to admit of the above specified classification, then, and in that case only, the paupers shall be classed as follows:—

1. Men, and youths above seven years of age.
2. Women, girls, and children under seven years of age.

Secondly. If for any special reason it shall at any time appear to the majority of the Board of Guardians, to be desirable to suspend the above rule, on behalf of any married couple, being of the aged and infirm class, the Guardians shall be at liberty to agree to their having sleeping apartments by themselves, detached from

THIRD, OR FOURTH CLASSES.

Fifthly. The children of the FOURTH CLASS shall be placed either in a ward by themselves, or in such of the wards appropriated to the female paupers as the Board of Guardians shall direct.—The mothers of such children to be permitted to have access to them, at all reasonable times.—With the foregoing exceptions, no pauper of one class shall be allowed to enter the wards or yards appropriated to any other class.

XII. The paupers of the several establishments comprised in the Union, shall be employed in any work which may be needed, and of which they may be capable, for the use of any or all of the establishments within the Union, or in any other way the Board of Guardians may direct.

DISCIPLINE AND DIET.

XIII. All the paupers in the workhouse, except THE SICK, THE AGED AND INFIRM, AND THE YOUNG CHILDREN, shall rise, be set to work, leave off work, and go to bed at the times mentioned in the accompanying table, marked A., and shall be allowed such intervals for their meals as therein are stated; and these several times shall be notified by ringing a bell; and during the time of meals, silence, order, and decorum, shall be maintained.

XIV. Half an hour before the bell shall have been rung for rising, the names shall be called over in the several wards provided for the FIRST, SECOND, and THIRD CLASSES, when every pauper, not being aged or infirm, belonging to the ward, must be present, to answer to his or her name, and to be inspected by the master or matron.

XV. No pauper of the FIRST, SECOND, OR THIRD CLASSES, except the aged or infirm, shall be allowed to go to or to remain in his or her sleeping-room, either in the time hereby allotted for work, or in the intervals allowed for meals, except by permission of the master.

XVI. As regards AGED AND INFIRM PERSONS AND CHILDREN, the master and matron of the workhouse shall (subject to the directions of the Board of Guardian) fix such hours of rising and going to bed, and such occupation and employment as may be suitable to their respective ages and conditions.

XVII. The meals for THE AGED AND INFIRM, THE SICK, AND CHILDREN, shall be provided at such times and in such manner as the Board of Guardians may direct.

XVIII. The boys and girls who are inmates of the workhouse shall, for three of the working hours at least every day, be respectively instructed in reading, writing, and the principles of the Christian Religion, and such other instructions shall be imparted to them as are calculated to train them to habits of usefulness, industry, and virtue.

XIX. The diet of the paupers shall be so regulated as in no case to exceed in quantity and quality of food, the ordinary diet of the able-bodied labourers living within the same district.

XX. No pauper shall be allowed to have or use any wine, beer, or other spirituous or fermented liquors, unless by the direction in writing of the medical officer, who may also order for any individual pauper such change of diet as he shall

extinguished. She had also to see that all paupers had clean linen and stockings once a week and all beds had clean sheets once a month; supervise washing and drying, making and mending; check the linen; oversee the care and diet of the sick and young children, the cleaning of the wards and all other parts of the premises, and enforce the "observance of good order, cleanliness, punctuality, industry and decency of demeanour among the paupers".

The first master and matron of the new workhouse were Mr and Mrs John Baker of

Fig. 7 - ULVERSTON WORKHOUSE FROM MILL DAM LATE 1800s

Ulverston, who were appointed in 1838 at a joint salary of £80 per annum, with lodging and maintenance "of such provisions as are in common without stint as to quantity". Their term of office was short, however. Mr Baker was dismissed in April 1839 for using "disrespectful language and demeanour towards the Board" when he was reprimanded for leaving the workhouse in the evening and not informing anyone of his whereabouts.

Mr and Mrs James Slater, a young couple under thirty years of age, were appointed as the new master and matron in May 1839. They were still in office in 1841. Despite their youthfulness, the Slaters ran the workhouse with just the help of a nurse and a porter and, of course, the female inmates who were conscripted into nursing and housework. Later, the staff was increased to include a schoolmaster, a schoolmistress and a tailor. Clothes were made in the house, if at all possible. Initially, inmates were made to wear a velveteen badge on the outside of their clothing, but this practice was discontinued in April 1840 at the instigation of the guardians. Thomas Gregg, the tailor shown in the 1851 census, was first an inmate in 1841. He died in the workhouse in 1873, aged 60 years.

Fig 8 - ULVERSTON WORKHOUSE DIET - 1839

BREAKFAST:

Sunday, Tuesday, Thursday,
Friday and Saturday:

Milk Porridge (3ozs. Oatmeal + 1pt Milk)

Monday and Wednesday:

Water Porridge (5ozs. Oatmeal +
1oz. Treacle or $^1/_2$ pt Milk)

DINNER:

Sunday: 5ozs. Meat + 2lbs. Potatoes

Monday: 5ozs. Bacon or Fish + 2lbs. Potatoes

Tuesday: 2ozs. Meat (to make $1^1/_2$ pts. Soup) +
6ozs. Oatcake

Wednesday: 5ozs. Bacon + 2lbs. Potatoes +
$3^1/_2$ ozs. Rice or Barley and $^1/_2$pt. Milk

Thursday: As Tuesday

Friday: 3ozs. Meat (for Sauce) + 2lbs. Potatoes

Saturday: As Monday

SUPPER:

Sunday: Water Porridge (5ozs. Oatmeal +$^1/_2$pt
Milk or 1oz Treacle)

Monday: Milk Porridge (3ozs.Oatmeal + 1pt Milk)

Tuesday: As Sunday

Wednesday: As Monday

Thursday: As Tuesday

Friday: As Tuesday

Saturday: 2ozs. Cheese + 6ozs. Oatcake

Out of the 5ozs. cooked meat on Sundays, any bones to be used for Soup on Tuesdays (to be included in the weight of the meat for that day). Bread could be given with porridge at breakfast and supper by using part of the meal allowed for the porridge to make the bread. The elderly were to be allowed 1oz. tea and 7ozs. sugar per week and 4ozs. 'household' bread per day. Children under nine years to have porridge and dinner 'allowed in proportion to their age'. [Note: N.H.S. Dietitian considers this diet to be boring but not necessarily a bad one. It provides 2,400 Calories per day: 13% from Protein, 28% from Fat, 57% from Carbohydrate; Iron content: 17mg, mostly from oatmeal; Vitamin C: 57mg, mostly from potatoes; Folic Acid: 256mg per day, mostly from oatmeal and potatoes – its main deficiency is that it contains no fruit or vegetables, other than potatoes.]

(Ref: Ulverston Union Guardians' Minutes 28.02.1839: PUU/1/2 – Barrow Record Office)

Fig 9 - POPULATION OF THE WORKHOUSE 1841-1901
composition at each census

	Total Inmates	Inmates Over 75	Children under 16	Unmarried women with children	Disabled	Imbeciles
1841	168	7	75**	*	0	0
1851	112	1	52	11	0	4
1861	218	18	93	27	1	12
1871	198	17	80	12	3	10
1881	255	34	79	12	3	18
1891	185	23	62	7	1	11
1901	219	25	57	6	1	3

*   *No marital status shown in Census*
**   *One girl (15) with a baby*
(Ref: Extracted from Census Returns – CRO Barrow-in-Furness)

Fig 10 - NUMBERS OF CHILDREN AND UNMARRIED MOTHERS
WITH CHILDREN
RESIDENT IN ULVERSTON WORKHOUSE 1841-1901

Census	U/M Mothers	Age Range	Their Children Under 16 yrs	Age Range	Children Without Parent/s	Total Inmates under 16 yrs.	Total of Inmates Local Born
1841	*				30**	75	80.8%
1851	11	20-40 yrs	16	3wk-15 yrs	25	52	94.6%
1861	27	18-45 yrs	43	4ds-13 yrs	33	93	80.0%
1871	12	20-42 yrs	20	6m-12 yrs	41	80	65.1%
1881	12	21-42 yrs	25	1 yr-14 yrs	23	79	65.5%
1891	7	22-52 yrs	13	1m-14 yrs	44	62	78.0%
1901	6	18-40 yrs	8	3m-12 yrs	37	57	58.0%

*   *No marital status is shown on the 1841 Census*
**   *One of the girls (aged 15) with a baby*
(Ref: Extracted from Census Returns CRO Barrow-in-Furness)

The medical officers attended to the parish paupers and had to appear before the Board to account for their patients whenever called upon by the guardians. The medical officer for Ulverston, John Postlethwaite, also attended to the sick in the workhouse and for this he was awarded an extra £5 per year (in 1839). He had to attend when sent for by the master or matron in case of sudden illness, accident or emergency, or as necessary for the treatment of the sick. He examined the paupers on admission and had to ascertain the cause of death of those who died within the workhouse. He advised on diets for the sick and provided any necessary medicines. He kept a register of the "sickness and mortality" of the inmates he treated, as well as making a weekly return to the Board of every attendance he made.

A resident nurse dealt with day to day complaints and illness. In July 1845, Margaret Braithwaite was appointed at £15.2s.0d. per annum, plus rations. Two chaplains were appointed in January 1839 – Rev. Richard Gwillyn was given charge of the female inmates and was expected to give prayers and a lecture on one day in the week; Rev. William Dodgson ministered to the male inmates and performed Divine Service in the House on Sundays. Both were attached to St Mary's Parish Church and initially received no salary, but in 1840, Rev. John Park received £15 per quarter. The chaplains were required to visit the sick paupers when requested and administer the Sacrament once every three months, on request. As much furniture as it was possible to re-use was removed from the old parish workhouses and, in November 1838, it was resolved that "all the bedsteads which can be removed from the workhouses at Ulverston, Colton and Dalton, be taken to a shipyard and boiled before they be received into the new workhouse". However, the shipyard refused to boil the beds and so they were cleansed with chloride of lime. New iron bedsteads were ordered from Bristol: 80 double and 20 single. Also 57 single and 102 double coconut fibre mattresses and 261 pillows. How these were transported from Bristol to Ulverston is not known, but possibly by sea.

Whilst advocating a diet which would provide enough nourishment for health and stamina (for work), the commissioners insisted that it should "be so regulated as in no case to exceed in quantity and quality of food, the ordinary diet of the able-bodied labourers living within the same district". The diet proposed by the guardians in 1839 is shown in Fig 8, but the commissioners objected on the grounds that it contained too much "animal food".

In the event of a death, there were reciprocal arrangements with other Unions to pay for all paupers' funerals, irrespective of settlement* considerations. The amount spent was strictly limited, however, and the service put out to tender. In 1837, the cost of a child's funeral was 12s. and 18s.6d. for an adult. By 1871, the cost had risen to £1.9s.6d. for a child under ten years old and £2.2s.6d. for an adult. Due to escalating costs, the earlier practice of burying inmates in their old parish was discontinued, unless funded by the family, and ultimately all burials took place at Holy Trinity Church or Ulverston Cemetery. Evidence of the dangers of accepting the lowest tender for such sensitive work is recorded in the guardians' minutes of 1881 when a Mr John Thompson complained that a parish coffin made for his granddaughter, a child, "had not been sufficiently deep".

*The township or parish to which a person belonged was their place of 'settlement' and, until 1865, each township or parish was responsible for its own paupers' expenses.

The stringent housekeeping that would allow such a dreadful thing to occur is evident in all of Ulverston Workhouse's written records - every penny was accounted for in careful detail. However, throughout its existence, the board of guardians appeared to be diligent in its duties, conforming to the rules and regulations imposed from London.

Fig 9 shows the composition of the workhouse population from 1841 to 1901. At times the system strained under the weight of these dependants and could not cope, especially as the increasing industrialisation of Dalton and the development of Barrow caused a huge population explosion in the area. As can be seen in Fig 10, a large proportion of inmates were children under 16 years without parent(s), the next largest were those with mother only. There were very few with father only.

As early as January 1878 an official report by inspector J.S. Davy recommended increasing the size of the workhouse, yet, despite serious overcrowding in the winter of 1881, plans for a new building to accommodate 140 persons, plus new laundry, piggeries, dead house and other outbuildings were turned down by the Local Government Board (which had replaced the Poor Law Commissioners). They suggested instead building a school for the children. New children's quarters were eventually built and plans, dated 1897, show two conjoined blocks each of three storeys, containing dormitories and attendants' rooms, workrooms and shared dining hall and kitchen. This relieved the pressure on the main workhouse block, as did the building of High Carley Hospital (designated a pauper fever hospital) in 1884.

Unfortunately, there are many missing documents and gaps in the records that survive of Ulverston Workhouse, making it difficult to build up a picture of everyday life within the house. The most comprehensive are the many volumes of minutes taken at the board of guardians' meetings and these have been used extensively in the following study, together with the master's report book, apprentice register, registers of births and deaths and visiting committee reports. Using all of these sources, this study gives some idea of what life was like for a small number of the many children who found themselves, for one reason or another, in the record books of Ulverston Workhouse during the reign of Queen Victoria.

In 1838 Ulverston was the largest town within the Ulverston Union; Barrow was still a hamlet within the parish of Dalton, and Dalton itself hardly more than a village. The children living within the Ulverston Union were, therefore, mainly village children whose families would have been involved in agriculture, perhaps with some small-scale quarrying or mining to supplement their income. They were not considered to be as deprived as the pauper children of the cities who were subjected to such dreadful poverty during the 19th century and would probably have had a healthier appearance than those "pale, hollow-cheeked" children observed by Nathaniel Hawthorne on his walks through the streets of Liverpool in the mid-1800s. Despite this, many villagers suffered intense poverty. However, where previously they had received poor relief in their own homes, the majority were now forced to enter the Workhouse.

It is not hard to imagine what effect entry into the workhouse would have had on a young child used to the close-knit community of the village. The building's high walls signified its separation from the rest of the town and its stark interior must have appeared huge and intimidating to those used to life in the cramped confines of a small cottage. Added to this, and probably the most daunting, was the separation from parents and siblings. If above seven years of age, they were forced to deal with this new environment without family support. The orphan child may have been better prepared for life in an institution after living in the village poorhouse, but the sheer size of the place would probably have intimidated even the hardiest of characters.

What these children would not have, until they left the workhouse, was freedom. Once inside its walls, their young lives were regimented and controlled and they exchanged the open fields for small yards, where exercise would be limited to walking in an orderly fashion.

Some indication of the surroundings in which these children found themselves can be gleaned from an undated inventory book, which showed only basic furniture. The boys' day room, for instance, had a table, cupboards and a "guard" – presumably a fire-guard, and the girls' was similarly bleak with a cupboard, forms, tables and "maidens" (for drying or airing clothes). There was no furniture in the bedroom, just beds, and some of these may have been shared (which would explain the large number of double beds initially ordered). The dining room contained only tables and forms.

All but the youngest were expected to attend Divine Service in the house every Sunday; only those who belonged to another religion (usually R.C.) were excused. The Regulations specified that children should receive three hours' instruction each day from the Chaplain, to include reading and writing and religious instruction "calculated to train them to habits of usefulness, industry and virtue". As no schoolmaster or schoolmistress is shown in the 1841 census, this was probably the only schooling given in the house at the time – although some children must have attended school outside, as the 1840 Standing Orders state: "the children going to the National School and those taught in the House shall be allowed paper and pens".

By the time of the 1851 census, there was a resident schoolmaster and a schoolmistress, but in 1881 no schoolteachers were resident. By 1891, there were two "industrial trainers", one man and one woman; they may only have taught the boys gardening and the girls domestic chores.

Not all of the children shown in Fig 9 as having no parent with them at the time of each census would have been orphans. A widow, or widower, may leave their child or children behind in the workhouse whilst they went in search of work. Those who found live-in work "in service" would not be able to take a child with them. Some of the children had a parent or parents in prison or in hospital, as in the case of Louisa Palmer, who had been in the workhouse alone since she was a year old. Louisa's mother was in the County Asylum and both were the subject of removal orders in 1862 from Dalton parish to one in Gloucester (their place of settlement), when Louisa was two. Similarly, Mary Backhouse of Hampstead, London, pleaded illness for not being able to take her child out of the workhouse, but she was made to remove the child within two weeks. Mary Nevinson's three illegitimate children were left in the workhouse when their mother was sent to prison in 1862.

There are several instances of families being resident in the workhouse over the period 1839 to 1901, but the greatest number of children were either illegitimate or orphaned. Fig.9 also shows the number of unmarried women with children at the time of each census. A "Lying-in Ward" was one of the features of the workhouse, yet it could not have been the safest of places in which to give birth. In 1870, when one infant in seven died in England and Wales , three out of eleven died in the workhouse in that year, higher than the national average . The guardians' minutes of January 1839 showed bluntly: 'Bastards chargeable to the Union at the end of Christmas Quarter:1836 – 157; 1837 – 72; 1838 – 68', and, in April 1863: 25 women with 40 illegitimate children in the workhouse. The total between 1858 and 1868 was 185 mothers with 294 illegitimate children – at a cost to the Union of £3,127.

Within one month from the day of the birth, the mother of each surviving illegitimate child born in the workhouse had to attend a meeting of the board to give evidence of paternity and then an affiliation order would be taken out against the father at the Petty Sessions. In May 1839, Catherine Armistead and Margaret Ashburner had the dubious distinction of being the first to go before the board under this rule.

14

How long the mothers and children stayed in the workhouse varied. Some names keep reappearing and many of the children knew no other home. Hannah Shaw appeared first in the census of 1871, aged thirty-two years, unmarried and with two children: Mary J., eleven years, and John, just one year old. In February 1875, her name is in the punishment book for persisting in using "disgusting language" to the matron and cook. She was taken before the magistrates, but because she was pregnant, escaped punishment. Her daughter, Alice, was born shortly after and is listed in the censuses of 1881 and 1891, along with her mother (Hannah, alone, in 1901). John, born in the workhouse, died there in April 1873, aged three years. Mary J. followed in her mother's footsteps and appeared several times in the punishment book – also for using "profane language" – and once, in 1884, with her mother, for fighting with another woman. For that offence, they each got fourteen days hard labour.

Another unmarried mother, Mary Ann Fell, was in the Workhouse in 1861, aged thirty-one years. She had four children with her, Margaret, eight years, Richard, seven, Robert, five and Eliza, ten months. Margaret died in 1869 aged seventeen and baby Eliza when she was two years old. In the census of 1861, Mary Ann gave her occupation as 'Drawer in Cotton Mill' and this gives a clue as to her reduced circumstances – in 1835 there were four cotton mills in Ulverston district, but by 1861 there was just one left. In 1871, Mary Ann was again in the workhouse, aged forty-two, still unmarried and with three more children: William, eight, Mary Ann, five and Margaret J., just one year old. By this time the older boys would have been put to work and the presence of the three youngest indicates that she must have lived outside the workhouse in the intervening years. She is there, alone, in 1881 and 1891. William is in the punishment book in 1875 and 1876. In 1877, aged fourteen, he was apprenticed to a tailor – from whom he absconded in 1881.

Attempting to strike a balance between costs and complying with Government regulations as to nourishment, the diet of the inmates was continually tampered with. In 1868, there were complaints of "too much water in the children's milk and too little bread in it" and, in 1873, the medical officer refused to sanction a diet of pease pudding and bacon for the children. Again, in 1879 the medical officer asked permission to alter the children's diet because of concerns over recurrent outbreaks of skin disease. The Local Government Board agreed, but thought that the cause of the complaint was as much due to "the unsatisfactory and overcrowded state of the workhouse". Perhaps the oranges, occasionally donated by local benefactors, would have helped if they had been a regular part of the children's diet.

The large number of children generally resident in the workhouse must have caused difficulties with discipline and order. Boredom must also have been one of the worst problems. In their dismal surroundings, with exercise taken in small, confined yards, there could have been no stimulation and no outlet for high spirits or childish games, just supervised walks with the schoolmistress in fine weather. On occasion, the children were invited to join in outside activities – such as the annual Town Bank Sunday School outing to Grange. Only at Christmas was there any attempt to provide entertainment in the house, together with gifts or invitations from outside patrons.

In 1885, J.R. Mozley, Inspector of Poor Law Schools, asked for bats and balls and skipping ropes and, again, in 1890: "materials for play for boys and girls", as none were left from presents given at Christmas, and asked for cupboards to be provided where bats and balls and skipping ropes and dolls could be kept. From this, it would appear that the guardians gave very little attention to the children's need for play. It is hardly surprising, therefore, that given the monotony of their day, some of the children got into mischief.

Those attending school in the town had the opportunity to abscond – as in the case of William Fell and Hugh Kirk who in 1876 returned at 7.00 p.m. after leaving school at 4.00 p.m. In September 1892, Robert Gudgeon, nine years old, received three strokes of the birch for going missing from Thursday noon to Friday morning.

Minor misdemeanours were dealt with by the master, others, by the magistrates, who usually sentenced the adults to fourteen days in the House of Correction – as in the case of Mary Jane Shaw for using obscene language "to the annoyance of other inmates in the Bedroom". Not many girls appear in the punishment book and none for fighting, except Mary Jane, who must have been a particularly difficult case – perhaps due to her many years spent incarcerated in the workhouse.

Punishment by restriction of diet was normally reserved for adults, but the guardians must have lost all patience with Robert Gibson, aged fourteen, after a series of incidents in 1875 when he was in the punishment book several times for fighting with other boys, throwing stones at a boy and also breaking a window. He was dieted for 48 hours, on specific instructions signed by the Chairman, quoting Article 129 of the Poor Law of 1834. Robert was also sent to break stones "according to Article 99". In June, he was in trouble again for returning an hour late from a walk and had bread for dinner for one day plus two strokes of the cane. Six days later, he was hired to a farmer at Hobkinground, Broughton, but the following Martinmas he returned to the workhouse. Again, Robert had spent years in the workhouse – he appears in the census of 1871 with his sister, Ann, but with no parent shown.

Boys were usually given the cane on one, or both hands, though in September 1891, John Milburn, aged thirteen, was considered 'uncontrollable' and was remanded for seven days and ordered by the magistrates to go to an industrial school until he was sixteen years of age. John ended up in the Kirkdale Industrial Schools in Liverpool – which must have been punishment enough for any child.

Kirkdale Schools were "training" schools for orphans and, according to the registers the children were later employed primarily in the Lancashire collieries or cotton mills. They were situated in one of the most densely populated areas of Liverpool – with, in 1871, 32,549 people living in myriads of little streets, tenements and unsanitary courts, close to the docks and warehouses and a notorious prison where public hangings took place until 1891.

John returned to the workhouse in February 1892 and immediately absconded with another boy. They applied to enter Barrow workhouse, but were returned to Ulverston. (Barrow had separated from Ulverston and formed its own Union in 1876.)

Despite the unwelcoming atmosphere of the workhouse and its strict regimes, it appears that for many mothers and children it became a place of refuge when life on the "outside" became too difficult. Its sombre appearance and stark furnishings notwithstanding, it was a roof over their heads and there was a regular, if boring, diet. These mothers were, perhaps, the 'ins' and 'outs'- referred to by M.A. Crowther who used the workhouse to get poor relief when necessary for survival, but who were also useful as unpaid workers in the house.

Some of the children spent almost all of their childhood within the workhouse walls and must have been thoroughly institutionalised. However, they too were fed and clothed and given shelter, when the alternative would have been a life of wandering the streets, living as best they could, trying to find work. As can be seen in Fig 9, the highest numbers of child inmates were during the industrialised periods of 1861 to 1881, when many people moved into the area in search of work, though the largest number of children without either parent occurs in 1891 – were they left by parents moving away from the area looking for work or because they could no longer care for them?

As inmates of the workhouse, the children were under the care of the guardians and, once they were old enough, were found work – and, hopefully, left the workhouse for ever.

Fig 11 -
ULVERSTON
MARKET
CROSS
CIRCA 1860
© Cumbria
County Council

17

CHAPTER 4   WORK AND TRAINING

The Ulverston Poor Law Union Standing Orders of 28 March 1839 had suggested that the (in house) "picking of cotton waste might be advantageously applied to all cases of able-bodied persons as well as children" (though there is no evidence to show that the children were ever employed in this way). On 3rd June 1840, a Standing Order recorded that:

> *"all the orphan boys and girls above twelve years of age now in the workhouse be offered as apprentices and notices thereof published and that the orphan boys be found comfortable clothing at the expense of the parish or township to which they respectively belong during the term of their apprenticeships and the orphan girls till the ages of eighteen".*

This ruling would also apply to the children of the unmarried mothers and widows who were all "chargeable" to the Union. Fig 12 shows a typical form of indenture for John Postlethwaite Smith.

The children would have expected to be put to work and were probably glad to escape life in the house. Apprenticeships of children as young as eight years had once been commonplace throughout the area – indeed, in 1837, the Ulverston guardians themselves had apprenticed Aaron Akister, then eight years old. In 1851, outside the workhouse, children as young as nine years were working alongside their parents and siblings, as "cotton spinners" in the Backbarrow Cotton Mill and, at Sparkbridge, John Bolton, aged seven, worked with his sister, who was ten, and his mother in the cotton factory there. So, in or out of the house, orphans or not, all pauper children were expected to earn their living. However, where once they would have been employed locally, they were now sent as far afield as the Union stretched and sometimes, further.

Not until 1872, when the guardians' minutes recorded: "No child to be sent as apprentice under the age of thirteen years in accordance with the Workhouse Regulation Act of 1867", was there any attempt to set a minimum age for the employment of the workhouse children. Even after that date the Relieving Officers' register shows that boys younger than thirteen years were being hired. Girls were sent as servants for meagre wages - as in the case of Mary Eleanor Pool, twelve years old, in service in Ulverston for six months in 1862 at a wage of 9d. per week, plus the "usual clothing" (i.e. two outfits of clothes). Isabella Beeton described the "maid of all work" as "deserving of commiseration; her life is a solitary one and, in some places, her work is never done. She is also subject to rougher treatment than the house- or kitchen-maid, especially in her earlier career". (Fig 13 is a copy of an original medical certificate issued for Alice Ebb in 1866 showing her fit for employment.)

18

Despite this, the girls had more freedom than the boys as they went from place to place for shorter periods of time. Though checks were made as to the suitability of the person offering employment, there was less supervision. Unfortunately, more freedom meant that temptations were harder to avoid.

Hannah White, in the care of the workhouse since at least 1861 when she was eight, was sent as servant to a tea dealer in Ulverston at age fourteen in 1867 – a situation found for her by the Board. By July 1868, she had changed places and hired herself

---

Fig 12 - INDENTURE OF JOHN POSTLETHWAITE SMITH 1864

This INDENTURE made this 27th day of October in the year of our Lord One thousand eight hundred and sixty-four Between The Guardians of the Poor of Ulverston Union in the County of Lancaster of the first part and Isaac Hadwin of the Township of Broughton East and County of Lancaster being a person above Twenty-one years and carrying on the trade of a Tailor not as a Journeyman but on his own account of the second part ... WITNESSETH that the said Guardians according to the provisions of the statute in such Case made and provided and the order of the Poor Law Commissioners in this behalf now in force in the said Union do bind and put out John Postlethwaite Smith of the Parish of Dalton in the said Union being a poor child above the age of nine years, that is to say, the age of twelve years who can read and write his own name and now residing in the Workhouse of the said Union of Ulverstone as Apprentice to the said Isaac Hadwin to learn the trade of a Tailor and to work and live at Grange in the Township of Broughton East in the County of Lancaster for the space of Seven years ...
ANY BREACH OF Covenants on the part of Isaac Hadwin ... damages to be paid Forty Shillings ...
ELIZABETH SMITH mother of the above named JOHN POSTLETHWAITE SMITH
DO HEREBY express my consent to the above binding

Elizabeth Smith X her mark

Signed by Isaac Hadwin
Signed by John Postlethwaite Smith

The Common Seal of the Guardians was affixed to this Indenture at a Meeting of the said Guardians aforesaid by Thomas Ainsworth squire Presenting Chairman
In the presence of   John Soulby Sykes   Clerk
INDENTURE CANCELLED – 10TH JANUARY 1867

(Ref: BT/HOS/UU/2/8 – Barrow Record Office)

to a grocer. In 1871, she was back in the workhouse, unmarried, where her son, George Arthur, was born. Very few boys were sent into "service" – or, surprisingly, farming. Traditional industries were giving way to new.

Until 1845, employment in the area had been provided by the haematite mines or the slate quarries and agriculture. Once the railway into Furness was opened, industry increased around the Dalton ironfields and the High Furness slate quarries and Barrow port developed. At the same time, the cotton mills declined in the Ulverston area and some of these mills changed over to making bobbins for the cotton spinners of Lancashire. The increase in population of the workhouse in 1861 could perhaps be attributed to the closures of the mills and the displacement of itinerant cotton workers, though the percentage of local born inmates (i.e. within the Ulverston Union's district) was high (Fig 10).

The bobbin mills were sited in remote areas where there was access to the coppice woods and water power to run the machinery. These were areas of low indigenous population and workers had to be brought in to cope with demand. Young apprentices had long been a feature of the cotton industry and as the new bobbin-making machinery required only basic skills, children were found to be the ideal, low-paid workforce.

Before the workhouse guardians apprenticed or "bound" a boy to an employer, some consideration was given to his suitability for the work and the medical officer was asked to comment on his fitness. The working practices of the employer were also subjected to scrutiny.

The guardians carried out the legal requirements and once a boy was thought suitable, he was taken before the magistrates for legal indentures to be entered into; these bound him for seven years to his employer. The indentures would be cancelled if there were serious problems on either side. Often the unhappy boys simply ran away, or "absconded", and if efforts to find them failed, the indentures were cancelled in their absence. They worked six days a week with long hours, when demand was high – possibly as long as the notorious Backbarrow apprentices of the early 1800s (a Parliamentary Select Committee investigation in 1816 discovered that the Backbarrow cotton mill apprentices stood at work from 5.00 a.m. to 8.00 p.m., with just one half-hour break for breakfast and another for dinner. They were also expected to work night shifts when business was good. Many of these apprentices were as young as seven or eight years old and several were apparently crippled because of these harsh conditions). The apprentices' only "rest" day was Sunday and this was intended for religious and other instruction. When the mills were stopped through lack of water to run the machinery some boys were given other tasks, such as "peeling sticks" in the coppice wood, as the Relieving Officer found on one of his regular visits to Cunsey Mill in 1877. These children had few rights; it was a form of slavery for all of them, indentured or not.

Various Factory Acts from 1819 to 1891, reducing hours and improving the conditions of child workers, were designed primarily for textile factories and had little or no impact on the bobbin-making industry. These small, rural units were outside the sphere of the city factory inspectors. As late as 1864, children under the care of Ulverston Workhouse were being sent as servants or indentured apprentices with no minimum hours of work specified in the indenture document and, in the case of servants, no legal document whatsoever.

The register entitled "Relieving Officers' Visits to Young Persons: 1863-1879" contains the names of 136 boys and girls who were either in service or apprenticeships during that period with comments on the children and their employment. The register lists (see Appendix) only a small number of the children who were apprenticed whilst under the guardianship of Ulverston Union, including those sent from other Unions to work in the area. Boys from the overcrowded West Derby Union of Liverpool - where there were children in abundance, but little employment - are well represented amongst the apprentices and servants (Fig 14). Others, not included in this register, came from the Fylde and Salford, Lancashire. Almost all went into the bobbin mills. Once in the area, these children came under the jurisdiction of the

---

Fig 13 - MEDICAL CERTIFICATE ALICE EBB

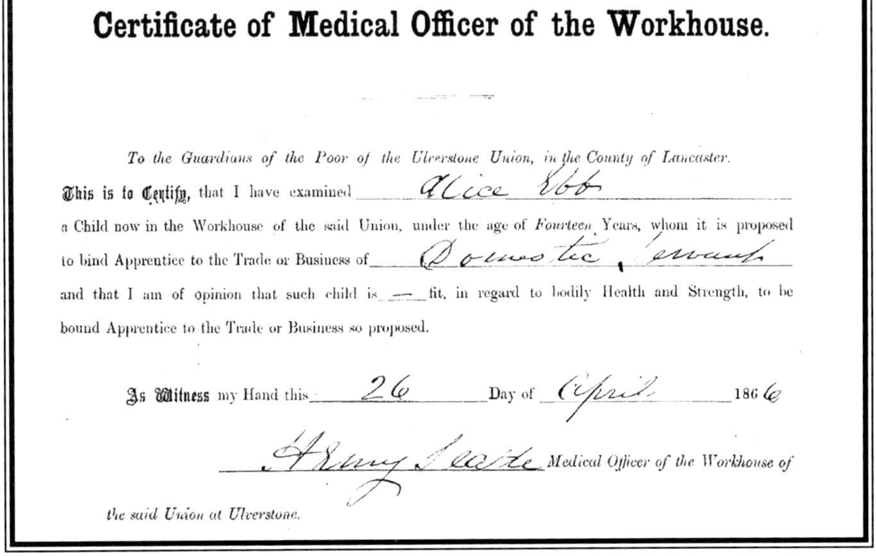

Certificate of Medical Officer of the Workhouse.

To the Guardians of the Poor of the Ulverstone Union, in the County of Lancaster.

This is to Certify, that I have examined _____ Alice Ebb _____

a Child now in the Workhouse of the said Union, under the age of Fourteen Years, whom it is proposed to bind Apprentice to the Trade or Business of_____ Domestic servant _____

and that I am of opinion that such child is ___ fit, in regard to bodily Health and Strength, to be bound Apprentice to the Trade or Business so proposed.

As Witness my Hand this_____ 26 _____ Day of _____ April _____ 186 6

_____ Henry Searle _____ Medical Officer of the Workhouse of the said Union at Ulverstone.

Ulverston Union. Under Article 66 of the Poor Law Orders, Ulverston guardians had to be informed of their placements. Crompton, in his "Workhouse Children", states that "after 1834 rural unions virtually ceased apprenticeships" – as can be seen, this was not the case in the Ulverston Union and, until 1899, there is no evidence of the guardians paying a "premium with each child to encourage an employer to take him", as stated by Crowther, only the usual "outfit of clothes".

Smith's indenture makes no mention of payments to the child, but in 1868 when Richard James Richardson was apprenticed to a blacksmith at Dalton, the guardians agreed an outfit of clothes, but also stipulated that Richardson was to receive 5s per annum for the first four years and 10s per annum for the last three years and in July 1873, approval of Indentures for Thomas Collinson included "pocket money" of 5s. for three years and 10s for the remainder, per annum. In August 1872, when the West Derby Union informed the Ulverston Board that it intended to place five boys at Cunsey Mill, the guardians wrote to West Derby stating that they objected due to: "the tender years of the boys, the arduous nature of the employment". Four of the boys were ten years old and one eleven. West Derby replied that they had visited Cunsey Mill on several occasions and had been thoroughly satisfied with the home which the boys had.

On 6th June and 20th June 1878, the local newspaper, Soulby's Ulverston Advertiser, printed details of the Ulverston Board of Guardians' meetings at which Mr Gibson, one of the guardians, entered his protest against boys being sent as apprentices to bobbin manufacturers. Mr Gibson likened the apprenticeships to seven years' penal servitude and said that the boys did not learn a useful trade and were "systematically ill treated and much neglected". A further article in the same paper in July 1878 quoted from the report prepared by the Clerk to the Union, in reply to Mr Gibson's allegations, with various statements on behalf of the bobbin manufacturers refuting Mr Gibson's claims.

The argument rumbled on and in December 1878, Major Alcock-Beck of Hawkshead, another guardian, asked for a Commissioner to enquire into the condition of apprentices and servants belonging to the Ulverston, West Derby, or any other Union, in respect of the "mode of hiring, their general treatment and instruction in the trade or employment" - presumably hoping to settle the matter once and for all. A letter to the Board from Mr Gibson (also sent to the Local Government Board in London), reiterated all of his previous complaints in detail and stated:

> *"We send them at twelve or fourteen for seven years without remuneration, there is no visiting committee, so that the boys are never seen from the time*

*they are sent unless they come back to the House. When their time is up they
are discharged (paupers) and some come back to the House again or take to
mining or labouring works and we send other boys to fill their places at the
Mills. They are in many cases...over-worked, half-clothed and fed and in
many ways very unfairly used."*

The apprentice register ran from 1863-1879, with one or two entries up to November
1881 - however, these later entries were few and incomplete. It was later revealed
that boys sent to James Robinson at Cunsey Mills and George Rushforth at Sunny
Bank, Torver, had no indentures, but were hired as "servants", having no legal status
whatsoever, though they were still bound for several years. A reply to a letter
received from the London Board was entered in the minutes on 3rd April 1879, as
follows:

*"In reply to your enquiries, I am directed to state that the number of boys
now under Indentures as bobbin turners is [left blank]. Also to state that there
are boys sent by the West Derby Union to Mr. James Robinson of Cunsey Mill
and to Mr. George Rushforth of Torver, in this Union – they are not under
Indenture, but as servants, etc. About three years ago a Special Committee of
the Guardians was appointed to enquire and report as to the treatment and
conditions of all the bobbin turners apprenticed and the boys from West Derby
as Servants and enclose a copy of the Report made to the Guardians on the
subject. [Report not in records]*

*"All the pauper apprentices and servants in this Union, whether apprenticed or
hired by the Guardians from this or sent by other Unions, have been regularly
visited by the Relieving Officers, who provide a Quarterly Report to the
Guardians and since the Committee's Report, above alluded to, the Board have
only had one or two complaints brought before them and which have received
their prompt attention.   (Signed) Devonshire, Chairman."*

Very few Ulverston boys were sent to Robinson's or Rushforth's Mills. The Guardians
favoured Stott Park Mill, Finsthwaite and Force Forge Mill, Satterthwaite for their
apprentices. Both of these mills were within the same area, to the south-west of
Lake Windermere. Stott Park Mill still exists and is now an English Heritage site. It is
situated in what must have been a very remote, wooded area, with the necessary
water to power the mill, and a cluster of cottages, which housed the bobbin master
and the young boys. The mill is stone-built with stone floors. The bobbin-making
machines were basic and required little skill to operate. The work must have been
boring and incessant, as demand was high. The operator of the blocking machine
was expected to make 1,000 bobbins a day . Fig 15 shows a young boy catching the
bobbins in a basket as they come out of the roughing machine. The unguarded

machines were dangerous - pieces of wood could fly off and cause injuries, especially to head or hands - and the workplace was covered in wood shavings, giving rise to respiratory disease (Fig 16). In winter, the wood shavings were allowed to accumulate on the floor, in order to provide some warmth – this must have created a huge fire risk, as lighting was by paraffin lamps in the early days. Sunny Bank Mill burned down in 1879. The business was removed to Cockermouth and three Ulverston apprentices moved with it. It appears to have been an unlucky mill – it was run by Michael J. Coupland until 1871, when he was declared bankrupt and his apprentices had their indentures cancelled.

As has been said, they were dangerous places to work. There is no record of Henry Croasdell having been employed in the bobbin mills, but, in 1871, aged sixteen, he had his hand amputated and the medical officer was requested to see he "be provided with an artificial hand or hook to enable him to work". However, John Dixon was working at Coward's bobbin mill at Skelwith Bridge when he received a serious head injury in July 1877. The relieving officer, James Dickinson, noted in the register that "This boy was severely injured on the head on July 28th – a sad wound – he is attended by Dr Harrison and every care is shown him by watching night and day". In October 1877, he recorded: "This boy has left, was injured on the head some time ago. He has recovered partially and now prefers some other work. Was not bound. The master states that he was a very fine boy. (At Dalton with an Aunt)". A brief note in the minutes in 1879 suggests that he may have returned to work: "John Dixon (15) to Jackson ... Bobbin Turner ... Bridge".

There were also those who succumbed to illness. Edward Harrison, apprenticed as a shoemaker in Barrow, returned to the workhouse in 1875 because of illness – his indentures were cancelled and Edward died in January 1876, aged fifteen. John Greaves, apprenticed to Isaac Myers, tailor of Beckside, Kirkby, died on 19th June 1871 whilst still indentured and is buried at Kirkby. In September 1872, John's brother, Arthur, replaced him at Isaac Myers' and, after completing his apprenticeship, worked for him "for some time after", according to the register. Another brother, James, was also apprenticed to a tailor, at Dalton – all three boys were in the workhouse in 1871, with no parent shown.

Not all placings worked out so well; John Purdie of West Derby complained of "ill usage" by Robinson of Cunsey Mill in 1868; James Croasdell and Thomas Latimer returned to the workhouse in 1878, with the consent of their master, Mr M. Walker of Force Forge Mill, and both parties "expressed dissatisfaction". Their indentures were cancelled on 6th February 1879. No explanation was given in the minutes. Both had complained of "scarcity of food" in 1876 and Thomas had constantly complained about his letters being opened. This was the second time Thomas's indentures had been cancelled, the first in 1873 when he worked for a plumber at

Fig 14 - TYPES OF EMPLOYMENT OF SERVANTS & APPRENTICES

TYPES OF EMPLOYMENT – BASED ON THE REGISTER OF RELIEVING OFFICERS' VISITS TO YOUNG PERSONS 1863-1879		MADE UP OF:	
Total Number Employed by:		ULVERSTON UNION:	102
BOBBIN MAKERS:	58	LIVERPOOL/WEST DERBY:	20 (one girl)
HOOPMAKERS:	4	STRATFORD-UPON-AVON:	2
CORDWAINERS/SHOEMAKERS:	11	KENDAL:	2
TAILORS:	24	NEWCASTLE-UNDER-LYME:	1
BLACKSMITHS:	7	BOOTLE, CUMBERLAND	1
BASKET MAKERS:	2	DUDLEY	2
PLUMBERS/GLAZIERS:	1	SOUTHPORT	1
PLUMBERS/PAINTERS:	1	CARLISLE	2
PAINTERS:	1	SCOTLAND	1
FARMERS:	3	IRELAND	1
TAILORS/INKEEPERS:	1		
SAILMAKERS:	1	(Ref: BT/HOS/UU/2/7 – Barrow Record Office)	
BLOCKMAKERS:	1		
TANNERS:	1		
HOUSEWORK: Girls 19/Boys	120		

Askam-in-Furness. Both of these boys were orphans.

Several complaints about food were made to the relieving officer on his visit to Stott Park Mill in July 1878. The master, in turn, complained about the conduct of some of the boys, particularly William Painter and William Lockley, both from Liverpool, and the master at Force Forge described Nicholas Bunting's conduct as "outrageous" in 1873.

Fig.15 - BOY 'CATCHING BOBBINS' 1899

Some boys were habitual absconders – often returning a few weeks, or months, later and settling back to work. Others disappeared completely and the police were often set to find them. Robert Mason absconded from his apprenticeship with John Parker of Kirkby and the Board ordered that Parker inform the Superintendent of Police. When Thomas Gibson ran away in 1879 and joined the army, the guardians were told that he had gone to Ireland with the 82nd Regiment - they did not attempt to get him back.

Whether any "absconders" got back home or not, is not known. (The burial registers of Holy Trinity Church, Ulverston for 7th September 1868 record three Fletcher brothers aged seventeen, eleven and nine "drowned on Ulverston Sands" – all workhouse children. Were they runaways? There is no mention of the incident in the guardians' minutes).

Fig 16 - BOY USING BORING MACHINE 1890
© Cumbria County Council

Others stayed, without trouble, and completed their apprenticeships. One such was Thomas Hughes who, in 1879, worked as a journeyman with Mr Robinson of Cunsey. Hughes was from West Derby and had never complained of his treatment, despite the Ulverston guardians' reservations about Cunsey Mill.

The large numbers of children in the workhouse, shown in the censuses of 1861, 1871 and 1881, caused the guardians to seek for solutions to the problem of overcrowding. In the 1860s and 1870s many charitable institutions, i.e. the Ragged School Union and Dr Barnardo's Homes , were springing up hoping to improve the lives of poor children and offering alternatives to life in the workhouse, known as "boarding out" into other parts of the community. One such institution was the Westmorland Orphans' Home in Kendal which, in 1872, offered six places to orphan

Fig 17- REPORT ON HOWARD HOME

13 Jun 1872   REPORT OF THE COMMITTEE APPOINTED TO INSPECT
THE WESTMORLAND ORPHAN HOME AT KENDAL:

Orphan Girls' Home in Kendal. Erected by the Hon. Mrs. Howard of Levens.
The Home was originally intended to be confined to the reception of destitute orphans of the County of Westmorland, but the 'benevolent Donor and Committee of Management, feeling satisfied of the superior advantages of the Home and living accommodation beyond the ascertained wants of the County of Westmorland'... (were offering places to other Unions)

The Home is vested in Trustees and the Committee of Management consists of the Hon. Arthur Upton, Revd. John Cropper, Vicar of Kendal, James Cropper, William Henry Wakefield, John Jowett Wilson, William Dilworth Crewdson, Esquires and John Whitwell, Esq., M.P.

The Home is situated about a mile from Kendal in the Milnthorpe Road and the House appears to have been erected with a view to securing to its fullest extent the health and comfort of the inmates; the rooms are spacious and lofty, well lighted and ventilated, the furniture good, clothing and general arrangements are all that can be desired. The healthy vigour of the girls, respectfully learning, cleanliness of person, suitable clothing, indicates the excellency of the management. There is a happy home-like feeling about the whole establishment, which it is in vain to look for in a Workhouse. All the work is done by the girls, no servants are kept. The Matron and Assistant direct and control, but beyond this all the household duties and the making and repairing of all their clothes are performed by the girls. The younger girls attend the Girls' National School in Kendal – the distance to walk to and from school gives healthy exercise. On very wet days the Matron keeps them at Home.

The girls are treated with confidence; none of the stores are locked, but there is no pilfering. They have their Playroom, toys and baskets, little articles in their bedrooms – as in a well ordered home.

Superior situations are provided for them in Service.

Mr. Cropper suggested that as a commencement six girls should be selected – they should be over 4 years and under 15 and prefer girls who have had as little of Workhouse life as possible.

The Charge to the Union : 2s.6d. per week plus 2 guineas (later confirmed as £2) each towards outfit when sent to Service and funeral expenses in case of death.

Prefer small numbers of girls, rather than the full number this Union could send. It is hoped that in time all orphan girls in the Union will be provided for in this Home.

As the charge made does not cover the cost of food, we venture to hope there may be amongst the benevolent of North Lonsdale, those who will be glad to assist a little in this good work.

(Extract from Ulverston Union Guardians' Minutes: C.R.O. Barrow-in-Furness Ref: PUU/1/12)

girls from the Ulverston Union. The guardians sent a representative committee to report on the home and, after their favourable report, six girls were chosen to be the first to enter this well-run establishment (Fig 17). In July 1872, Agnes and Margaret Briggs, aged ten and five, Jane and Isabella Croasdell, ten and seven, (sisters to Henry?) and Agnes Martin, ten, were admitted to the Orphan Home. Margaret Robinson, the sixth girl, did not join them until January following as in July she had "an eruption on her face". No doubt the threat of smallpox made the home cautious – smallpox was rife that year. Little Margaret Law Briggs unfortunately died at the home in December 1872 – an event given only a brief mention in the Ulverston Guardians' minutes.

In the orphanage, which later came to be known as "Howard Home", the girls were well looked after and taught respect, cleanliness of person and all the skills necessary to become a servant or nursemaid in the "superior situations" which were found for them.

Several more orphan girls were sent to the home and, in January 1873, Lucy Jacques (variously spelled Jacks/Jakes), arrived there and appeared to settle well, until, in August 1878, she and sisters, Elizabeth Ann and Dinah Butler, were transferred to the care of Kilburn Orphanage in London. Following a letter confirming their safe arrival, the Mother Superior immediately wrote again saying that "Lucy Jack's conduct was so strange and peculiar" that she was unsuited to be an inmate of that establishment and would be sent back. Lucy was born in the Ulverston Workhouse on 21st November 1866, daughter of William and Hannah Jacques of Holker Upper; Hannah died in the workhouse in 1870 and William in 1871. Lucy was returned to Ulverston in September 1878 and in the 1881 census she is still shown as an inmate and described as 'Imbecile' - but later was in the County Asylum.

The Howard Home took good care of the girls if there were problems with ill health or with losing a "place". Jane Croasdell had a period of illness, which necessitated her being admitted to Garlands Asylum in Carlisle, but she was last shown in the home's register working in Darwen, Lancashire in 1885. Her sister, Isabella, was in service in Bolton in the same year .

For those boys not yet old enough for work the solution to overcrowding appeared to be admission to the Swinton Industrial Schools – part of the Manchester Union. Originally charitable institutions, intended for children without home or guardian (or those out of control), industrial schools became the responsibility of the Committee for Education in 1870, and workhouses could send children who were unruly or disobedient. Whether the Ulverston boys sent to Swinton fitted this category is not known but several were sent there for training.

In April 1879, Mr Hall, medical officer for Dalton, had visited Swinton and reported very favourably on the treatment and appearance of the boys and their education.

Alfred Croker, an orphan, was sent there and in March 1879. Swinton informed the guardians that he was "fit to be placed to a trade". Unfortunately, Alfred must not have given satisfaction as, in October of the same year, Mr Ely of Tinsley refused to have him and "as he was not apprenticed he requested to send him back". This may have been due to Alfred being disabled; in 1873, when he was seven, part of his leg had been amputated, due to a "crippling disease of the knee".

There were thirteen Ulverston boys at Swinton schools in September 1879 and there was a suggestion to send girls there, due to overcrowding in the house (236 inmates on 16/10/1879). However, in January 1880, the manager at Swinton declared the schools full and they could take no more children from Ulverston - they already had fifteen. This appears to have caused something of a panic as overcrowding became more acute – in the previous November, the girls' ward was full and twenty-three boys were removed from the main house and placed in "the empty house at the top of the garden" in the care of one of the men.

The Clerk was instructed to write to Liverpool and Manchester in an attempt to find places for the children. In September, a letter was received from Liverpool Parish offering places at Kirkdale Industrial Schools (where John Milburn had been sent for his bad behaviour), at a cost of 4s.10d. per child, per week. It was resolved that three of the Ulverston guardians would visit the schools and report back. Then, a further letter from Swinton offered to take five more boys – thus making the full Ulverston complement allowed by the Local Government Board.

The report on the visit to Kirkdale Schools was "Satisfactory as to general character" and the board sanctioned sending thirty boys and twenty girls. However, a letter from the Government Board dated 29th October 1880 stated:

"I am directed to state that the Kirkdale Schools already receive children from the West Derby and Prescot Unions, as well as those belonging to Liverpool and as it is probable that the number of inmates which is very large at the present time will increase during the winter, the Board do not feel justified in sanctioning the admission of children from the Ulverston Union. The Board must therefore decline to assent to the proposal."

The clerk was instructed to reply, asking if a smaller number could be sent to Kirkdale Schools. Then, in December, the clerk wrote to Barrow to ask if they could take any of the children.

In December 1881, sixteen old men had to be transferred to sleep in the fever ward at the top of the garden, all beds were full in the women's wards and there were four more inmates in the house than allowed by the Government Board; despite this, they rejected the guardians' plans to extend the workhouse. As stated, they preferred a school be built. Presumably this was in anticipation of the new ruling in 1882 which stated that, in England children could not be legally employed full-time unless they had reached, or passed, the 4th Standard in school or, for half-time, unless they had reached the 3rd Standard. (The workhouse children attending Dale Street School in Ulverston were passing 5th and 6th Standards).

In 1882, Ulverston Union became "The Rural Sanitary Authority of the Ulverston Union" and, in 1884, the Guardians opened a new fever hospital for pauper patients at High Carley, outside Ulverston. The old fever hospital in the grounds of the workhouse could thus be used to relieve the pressure on the main house. This, and Barrow having its own Union, meant that, in 1884, the boys at Swinton could be brought back to Ulverston. The agreement with the Manchester Board was terminated, with thanks for the "great convenience the arrangement has been to this Board".

Settlements were still a problem, even in 1891. Six children were ordered to be removed from the workhouse to "their place of settlement" and on 4th July 1891, Joseph, aged thirteen, William, eleven, Martha, nine, Albert Edward, seven, Mary Elizabeth, six, and Annie Porritt, three, were admitted to Warrington Union. Their father, Albert Thomas Porritt, had presumably had them admitted to the workhouse when he went off to find work, or, as in so many cases, he may just have abandoned them.

Towards the end of the century, change was only very slight; girls were still being sent out as servants - though generally not until they were fifteen – at the only slightly increased wage of 2s. per week. Unfortunately, Ellen Young, sent as servant to Mrs Wilding, fish dealer, of Tyson Square, Ulverston in December 1891, was returned after only eight weeks for "breaking pots and telling lies". Out of the 16s. due to her, Ellen had to pay 6s. for the broken pots. At least Ellen got a wage, however small. In 1891 James Miller went "in service" to Mr Gilpin for pocket money and clothes - not so different to when Mary Parker was hired to Anthony Shepherd of Millom in June 1816 "for meat and close (sic) for three years". (Kirkby Ireleth Select Vestry Book)

The minutes record fewer boys being apprenticed to the bobbin mills by the time John Brittle, fourteen, was sent to Stott Park on one month's trial in 1891 – no doubt due to the gradual decline in the bobbin industry from the 1870s, when cotton manufacturers began producing their own bobbins. John was in the workhouse in

1881 with his mother, but alone in 1891. Whether he went on to be fully indentured is not known.

More prevalent were the short-term hirings to local tradesmen and farmers. In May 1893, Percy Slater was hired to Thomas Wood, butcher, at Lowick at £1 for half a year, plus an outfit, and Henry Tattersall and John Athersmith both got positions at £1 for half a year. John was hired to the Vicar of Colton to look after his pony and work in the garden and Henry to a farmer at Bardsea. Charles McCann went to Oxen Park for £2 for half a year, plus two shirts and two pairs of stockings. Many were not so lucky. In June 1892 George Dixon, aged sixteen, after working for Mr Leece of Cartmel for eight months, returned to the workhouse destitute – as, no doubt, would John Tattersall, fifteen, who was hired for only 10s. for a half year and James Machell, who was returned after twenty-six weeks as he was "too weak". These boys would be sent to the next hiring fair to, hopefully, gain another situation, otherwise it was back to the workhouse.

Though most of these hirings point to an untrained workforce destined for labouring jobs, there were exceptions: Walter Scott, in the workhouse at the time of the 1891 census, was apprenticed as a pupil teacher in October 1893 when he was thirteen or fourteen; John Miller, fifteen, was sent to Lloyd Parsons, electrical engineer of Cunsey in February 1893; and in 1899, the guardians requested special permission from the Government Board to subsidise the apprenticeship of a boy to an "Art Photographer and Printer", as the boy was "physically unfit to earn his own livelihood", but had shown a flair for drawing at school. The London Board agreed to the payment towards the boy's board and lodging for twelve months, initially, plus 6d. per week pocket money. In the same year, another similar request was made on behalf of Thomas Wilson, sixteen, to be apprenticed at an Ulverston boot factory. Again, London agreed as the boy was disabled due to hip joint disease.

There were also children in special schools for the deaf and dumb; Margaret Knipe was sent "home" to the workhouse for the Christmas holidays of 1891 from the Liverpool Deaf & Dumb School. She presumably travelled by train and was met at Carnforth by Mr Bell, a relieving officer. George Vickers was attending the Boston Spa Deaf & Dumb School in Lincolnshire when, in September 1898, the minutes recorded a letter from the school asking the Ulverston guardians for authority to supply him with a "hook" for the stump of his arm, which was amputated. George had already been placed by the school to learn the trade of sign writing; whether the loss of his hand pre-dated his placement is not specified.

Others were sent to the Bishop O'Reilly Memorial Schools in Leyfield, and Lostock Hall Industrial School near Preston. Emily and Margaret Polkinghorn went to the "Training Home for Friendless Girls" in Carlisle, at a cost of 4s. each per week, paid by the Ulverston Guardians.

In January 1899, four boys were sent to the new Training Ship "Indefatigable" in Liverpool Bay, which cost the guardians 7s. each boy per week, plus an outfit. Their ages ranged from twelve to fourteen years. 1888 and 1889 various notices were being received informing the guardians of schemes to send children out to Canada; there is no record of any child being sent from Ulverston.

By the end of the century there were, perhaps, signs of a little more kindness creeping in: small children were being considered for adoption; relatives were claiming their orphan nieces and nephews; the local benefactors brought magazines and books, toys for the children and flowers for the sick wards.

In 1891, there was an invitation for the children to go for an evening ride on the "Alpine Railway Station" in the Gill, Ulverston; there were fireworks for them in November 1892 and, in March 1898, the Kentucky Minstrels' show visiting Ulverston offered free tickets to workhouse children.

It is to be noted that these few "treats" were made possible by benefactors outside the house. The Kennedys of Stone Cross in Ulverston were constant benefactors and Mr. Kennedy was also a guardian. In July 1898, the children were invited to Stone Cross for tea and, in December 1899, to a "Christmas Tree Party" there. This was a remarkable advance in the acceptance of workhouse children, in contrast to 1838.

There was still stigma attached to the inmates, of course, and an example of the separation of "town" and "workhouse" occurred on the occasion of Queen Victoria's Diamond Jubilee in 1897 when the town children were each presented with a commemorative china mug and the workhouse children were given a cheaper enamelled tin replica (Fig 18). In fact Crowther states that the stigma of poverty had increased by the late 1800s, because, with improved standards of living, the working classes strove to emulate the middle classes. This would hardly apply to the children – for the orphans, at least, the workhouse would offer security and children without parent or relative, according to Crowther, made up half of all indoor pauper children throughout the 19th century.

Fig 18 - QUEEN VICTORIA JUBILEE MUG

The new Children's Department had been built behind the main house by 1897/8. It consisted of two particularly austere-looking buildings, which became known as "The Dales". However, they did at least ensure some separation from the more unpleasant aspects of the main house. Only through conjecture can we visualise the lives that the children led in close proximity to the diverse and shifting population of the workhouse; the constant "itch" (at one time so prevalent that it justified its own ward); the dust and noise of the stone-breakers, the smell of the adjacent piggeries and the "stinking privies" that were condemned in a Board of Health Report of 1855. Fig 19 shows the Dales in their derelict state, just before demolition in 2004, when their starkness was very apparent.

Ulverston Workhouse continued to operate for many more years after 1901 as a refuge for the elderly, orphans, unmarried mothers, the sick and insane and vagrants – in fact, all of those who were thought to pose a problem for society. Many of those categorised as "vagrants" were men who trailed from place to place looking for work, taking advantage of a night's lodging in the workhouse - this also applied to women and children. The institution was taken over by the Ministry of Health in 1919 and eventually became a geriatric hospital. The building, once the focus of so much activity, controversy and pain, a physical embodiment of a system that came to be reviled throughout the whole country, was demolished in 2004 to make way for a new health centre.

Fig.19 - "THE DALES" CHILDREN'S QUARTERS
Prior to demolition in 2004

CHAPTER 5   **CONCLUSION**

During the period 1838-1901, several hundred children must have passed through the Ulverston Workhouse system and, of course, it has not been possible to name all of them – many who are lost within the pages of the guardians' minutes remain to be found. Only a small cross-section has been featured here in an attempt to show what life in the workhouse was like for a child and under what conditions they lived in these 19th century institutions. It could be argued that, despite the stigma that entering the workhouse represented, there were advantages for those children who, through poverty and circumstance, were forced to live there.

The Ulverston board of guardians appears to have cared adequately for the children in its charge, though it dispensed its charity sparingly, with business-like efficiency, minimum compassion and no indulgence. As far as can be ascertained from the records, the children appear to have been clothed, fed, given a basic education and found employment. They also received necessary medical attention and were vaccinated to protect against smallpox. Their world may have been harsh, but the world outside the workhouse walls was equally so. The streets of the towns and cities in the 1830s and 1840s were full of impoverished children: an estimated ten thousand urchins roamed the streets of London in the mid-1800s and many of them ended in prison. As late as 1891, women and children are thought to have accounted for fifteen percent of casual applicants to workhouses.

It is most likely that many of the boys in the workhouse would have been unruly and difficult to handle, but punishment does not appear to have been excessive, although there is only the master's punishment book for evidence of that.. However, there is no reason to suspect there were any incidences of extreme cruelty as occurred at other workhouses. According to Engels, at Greenwich Workhouse, in the summer of 1843, a five year old boy was made to sleep on the lids of coffins in the "dead room", and, at Hearne, where the same punishment was used to discipline a little girl for wetting the bed. Such tales greatly increased the fear of the workhouse that was deeply ingrained in the poor.

The bad working conditions experienced by children, particularly in the cotton mills and woollen mills throughout the north of England, resulted in many outspoken criticisms from those with power to sway public opinion and such campaigns eventually forced legislative and social changes. These changes had at first only a minimal impact on the lives of workhouse children, but the

Education Act of 1870, giving every child the right to some form of schooling, was a most important development. The advent of philanthropists such as Dr Thomas J. Barnardo, who opened his first children's home in 1870, and Thomas B. Stephenson, the Methodist minister who founded what was to become the National Children's Home, and many others, meant that attitudes towards destitute children slowly began to change.

In conclusion, it has to be said that, in the Workhouse or out, no satisfactory solution was found to combat the extreme poverty of the time and not until very much later were the needs of all pauper children specifically addressed, but not necessarily resolved.

J.H.Whitehead 2005

Appendix:
Details of the Apprentices listed in the Ulverston Union Relieving Officers' Register 1863-1879

Barrow Record Office Ref: BT/HOS/UU/2/7

ALCOCK, Edward   from Stratford-upon-Avon
Hired: 10.05.1875 (age 13)
Employer: Force Forge Bobbin Mill
July 1878:   "No water to run the mill."

ATKINSON, George
Hired: 14.07.1870 (age 14)
Employer: Daniel Braithwaite, Cordwainer, Hindpool, Barrow
Oct.1871:   "No complaint. Attends Barrow Church regularly" (R.O. George Simpson)

BARROW, John
Hired: 02.02.1871 (age 12)
Employer: Michael J. Coupland, Sunny Bank Mill, Torver. Bobbin Turner.
July 1871:   "Master is Bankrupt and Indentures are cancelled."

BORWICK, John William Parker   b. Ulverston
Hired: 22.01.1863 (age 13)
Employer: Matthew & Henry Walker, Force Forge. Bobbin Turner.
Nov. 1867:   "No complaints. Attends Satterthwaite Chapel."
April 1870:   Out of Apprenticeship (age 19)
1861 Census: In workhouse *[with mother, Frances (32) U/M, b. Subberthwaite*
brothers: Daniel (8) and Robert (5)]
Oct. 1862   Was on sick list – sent to Force Forge on trial :
15.01.1863:   Indentures agreed: *[In G.Mins. named as William John Parker Barwick. He was on the sick list when first considered for*
apprenticeship and it was deferred for two months until M.O. said he was fit.]

BELL, Thomas Taylor
Hired: 15.11.1863 (age 13)
Employer: Peter Carter, Backbarrow. Hoopmaker.
Oct. 1867:   "No complaints. Attends Backbarrow Chapel." (R.O. Roger Taylor, jr)
April 1870:   "Removed from the District"

BIBBY, Thomas
Hired   09.01.1864 or 65 (age 12)
Employer: Hugh H. Towers, Force Forge Bobbin Mill.
Nov. 1867:   "Attends Satterthwaite Chapel."
Oct. 1871:   Apprenticeship expired

BIBBY, James
Hired: 18.04.1867 (age 13)
Employer: Hugh H. Towers, Force Forge Bobbin Mill.
Nov. 1867:   "No complaints. Attends Rusland Church"

BOLTON, John Walter   from West Derby Union, Liverpool
Hired: 03/06/1875 (age 10)
Employer: Jos. Robinson, Cunsey Bobbin Mill.
Oct. 1876:   "Requested to be moved back to West Derby Union" (R.O. Jas Dickinson)
Jan. 1877:   "This boy asked last visit to be removed but now wishes to stay, is looking better in health, etc. Attends day school half time."
Apr. 1877:   "Found the mill stopped and was told by Mrs. Robinson that the boys were peeling sticks in a coppice wood at some
             distance.

BOWMAN, John Solomon
Hired: 24.06.1867 (age 11)
Employer: Thomas Baynes, Tailor, King Street, Ulverston.
Sep 1867:   "No complaints. Attends Independent Chapel." (R.O. Jas Riley)
Jly 1874:   "At his trade. This young person is now a Journeyman."

BRAITHWAITE, John Thomas
Hired: 15.12.1870 (age 14)
Employer: George Braithwaite, Sailmaker, Sunderland Terrace, Ulverston.
01.04.1871: "No complaints. Attends New Church." (T.O. Jas. Riley)
Jan 1872:   "Indentures cancelled – gone elsewhere."

BROCKBANK, John Thomas
Hired: 16.11.1871 (age 13)
Employer: John Jackson, Blacksmith, Gleaston.
Jly 1872:   "No complaints. Attends Dendron Chapel." (Geo. Simpson)
1878:   "Apprenticeship expired and left."

BROCKBANK, Laurence   (also Lawrence)
Hired: 22.02.1867 (age 11)
Employer: John Wilkinson, Tailor, Swarthmoor
Sep 1867:   Indentures cancelled (R.O.James Riley)
Hired: 08.02.1868 to William Pawson, Dalton, Cordwainer
Visit: "Quite satisfactory. Attends Dalton Church regularly." (R.O. G.Simpson)
Hired: 12.11.1869 Indentured to James Nelson, Church Stile, Pennington. Blacksmith.
Visit: "No complaints. Attends Pennington Church."
Hired: 12.11.1870 (age 15) to Jos. Murthwaite, Bouth, Blacksmith.
Jan 1871:   "No complaints. Attends Independent Chapel" (R.O. Jas Riley)
Oct 1871:   "No complaints. Attends Colton Church."
Oct 1872:   "Not with his Master." (R.O. Taylor) *[In May 1863 Laurence's aunt applied to the Guardians to take Laurence (age 7) out of the house for a fortnight.]*

BROWN, Michael   from West Derby Union, Liverpool.
Hired: 23.09.1878 (age 12)
Employer: Joseph Robinson, Cunsey Bobbin Mill.
27.09.1878: "Had absconded 2 days prior to my visit. Attempted twice before." (R.O. Jas. Dickinson)
Jan 1879:   "Not yet heard of."

BUNTING, Nicholas
Hired: 26.01.1870 (age 15)
Employer: Force Forge Bobbin Mill, Satterthwaite.
Jun 1873:   "Master complains of his outrageous conduct. Attends Church at times."
Oct 1874:   "Quite satisfactory. Attends Rusland Chapel." (R.O. Jas Dickinson)

BURNS, Elizabeth
Hired: 06.12.1866 (age 13)
Employer: Elizabeth Kendall, Grocer, The Weint, Ulverston.
Sep 1867:   "Has engaged herself elsewhere." (R.O. Jas. Riley)

CHARNOCK, Edward
Hired: 18.04.1867 (age 13)
Employer: Hugh Towers, Force Forge Bobbin Mill.
Nov 1867:   "No complaints. Attends Rusland Church."

CLARK, John
Hired: 16.09.1869 (age 11)
Employer: Joseph Comber, Tailor, Paxton Street, Barrow.
Oct 1869:   "Quite satisfactory. Attends Barrow Church."(R.O. G. Simpson)

CLARK, Thomas   b. Dalton
Hired: 13.05.1872 (age 13)
Employer: Thos. Mashiter, Tailor & Draper, King Street, Ulverston.
Jan 1873:   "No complaints. Attends Old and New Church." (R.O. Jas. Riley)
06.10.1876: "This young man is now working for himself, his Master having become bankrupt."
1871 Census: In workhouse.

CLARKE, Richard   from Liverpool
Hired: 24.12.1873 (age 14)
Employer: W. & J. Coward, Stott Park Bobbin Mill.
Jan 1874:   "Satisfied. Attends Church regularly." (R.O. John Nicholson)
12.07.1878: "Complains about food. Masters not satisfied by his conduct (age 19)."
Jly/Aug 1878: "Absconded"

CLARKE, Robert   from Liverpool
Hired: 13.02.1873 (age 13)
Employer: Stott Park Bobbin Mill, Finsthwaite.
Apr 1873:   "Attends Finsthwaite Chapel. No complaints." *[Were Robert and Richard one and the same or were they brothers?]*

37

COLERIDGE, Gildart (Gilbert)
Hired: 14.09.1876 (age 15)
Employer: Ed. Borwick, Ferry Hotel.
10.12.1878   Rushforth's Sunny Bank Bobbin Mill
12.02.1879   "Bobbin Mill burned down. Removed with Master to Mills at Cockermouth"

COLLINSON, John   from Kendal Union
Hired: (age-)
Employer: Jackson Coward, Skelwith Bridge Bobbin Mill, Ambleside.
             08.08.1877 (age 20): "This youth wrote to the Board, complained of being struck by Master. He is now satisfactory."
July 1878:   Out of Apprenticeship.

COLLINSON, Thomas   b. Kendal
Hired: 24.07.1873 (age 12)
Employer: M. & H. Walker, Force Forge Bobbin Mill.
Aug 1873:   "Quite satisfactory. Attends Satterthwaite Church." (R.O. Jas. Dickinson)
Jly 1878:   "Complains at having only sawing work to do."
Nov 1878   "No complaints."
1871 Census: `In workhouse. [Thomas's Indentures were to include pocket money: 5s. for three years and 10s for remaining, per annum.]

CONDELL, William   (Also CRODELL)
Hired: 23.09.1878 (age 13)
Employer: Jos. Robinson, Cunsey Bobbin Mill.
Jan 1879:   "Quite satisfactory." (R.O. Jas. Dickinson) [G.Mins. 03.10.1878: Shown as William Crodell from West Derby Union]

COULTON, William
Hired: 29.12.1864 (age 11)
Employer: James Bland, Shoemaker, Grange.
Oct 1867:   "No complaints. Attends Grange Chapel."
Jan 1868:   "Deserted his Master."
1861 Census: In workhouse (7) [with mother, Elizabeth (31) U/M, from West Derby Union,
             brothers, John (4) and James (10m)]

COWARD, Alice
Hired: 04.06.1870 (age 14) - for Housework
Employer: William Todd, Butcher, Market Place, Ulverston
Oct 1870:   "No complaints. Attends New Church" (Holy Trinity)
01.04.1871: "Left her place. Returned to workhouse"
1861 Census: In workhouse [?with mother, Jane (46) wife of Gen.Lab., of Urswick.
?father, Robert (71) of Kirkby Ireleth.]

CROASDELL, James
Hired: 09.11.1870 (age 12)
Employer: Force Forge Bobbin Mill.
03.10.1876: "Complains of having a scarcity of food" (R.O. Jas Dickinson)
Dec 1878:   Returned to workhouse by masters (Walker's).
24.12.1878: Guardians cancelled his Indentures (age 20)
             [7 months before completion of his term]
             "Masters agreed to let him go on condition that they did not provide him
             with the usual suit of clothes. Indentures ordered to be cancelled by the
             Magistrates" (Ulverston Guardians' Minutes 24.12.1878.
1871 Census: [?brothers: Henry (15) b. Liverpool and James (13) b. Dalton.
? brother to Jane (10) and Isabella (7) orphans of Henry and Hannah who
were sent to Howard Home, Kendal in June 1872.]

CROKER, John
Hired: 11.01.1872 (age 13)
Employer: Thomas Melish, Cordwainer, Dalton.
Jly 1872:   "No complaints. Attends Independent Chapel Dalton." (R.O. Geo. Simpson)
27.04.1878: "His master has given him his Indentures and he has left his place."

DANSON, Myles
Hired: ? 1877
Employer: R. B. Creighton, Hooper, Backbarrow.
Jan 1878:   "Satisfactory. No complaints." (R.O. Jas. Swainson)
15.09.1879: "Satisfactory. No Complaints." (R.O. W. Storey)

DIXON, James
Hired: 14.09.1865 (age 12)
Employer: David Mawson, Tailor, Penny Bridge.
1867-1868:   "No complaints. Attends Penny Bridge Chapel" (R.O.R.Taylor,jr)
Oct 1872:   Apprenticeship expired.

38

DIXON, John
Hired: 18.04.1872 (age 13)   b. Bootle, Cumberland.
Employer: Joseph Sharpe, Blockmaker, Ramsden Street, Barrow.
Sep 1872:   "No complaints. Attends St. George's Church" (R.O. Roger Taylor)
03.02.1873   "Indentures cancelled"
1871 Census: In workhouse (12).

DIXON John James
Hired: 17.04.1873 (age 12)
Employer: M. & H. Walker, Force Forge Bobbin Mill.
Aug 1873:   "Quite satisfied. Attends Satterthwaite Church." (R.O. Jas Dickinson)
03.10.1876:   "Stockings have been supplied since last visit."
1871 Census: In workhouse (12). *[John and John James appear to be one and the same. His age on entering Force Forge Mill was put at 12 – this is the only difference between the two records.]*

DIXON, John
Hired: 01.01.1875 (age 11)
Employer: Jackson Coward, Skelwith Bridge Bobbin Mill.
28.07.1877:   "This boy was severely injured on the head on July 28th – a sad wound –
                he is attended by Dr.Harrison and every care is shown him by watching
                night and day." (R.O. Jas Dickinson)
31.10.1877:   "Left to Aunt at Dalton. Partial recovery."
30.12.1879:   Guardians' Minutes : John Dixon (15) to Jackson, Bobbin Turner, -Bridge. *[Apart from the discrepancy in age, this and the previous John Dixons could be one and the same, changing employers after short periods. The R.O's records contained many discrepancies with ages, date of hiring, etc.]*

DIXON, William
Hired: 30.10.1865 (age 14)
Employer: Thomas Dickinson, Basket Maker, Arrad Foot.
1867-1868:   "No complaints. Attends Penny Bridge Chapel." (R.O.R.Taylor,jr)
Oct 1872:   Apprenticeship expired.
1862 Census: In workhouse. *[Brother to James Dixon above and sister, Mary Jane; orphans of William Dixon of Ulverston. Aunts in Preston, Mrs. Livsey and Miss Casson.]*

EDMONDSON, Benson
Hired: 24.03.1870 (age 11)
Employer: Wm. & John Coward, Stott Park Bobbin Mill.
July 1870:   "No complaint. Attends Finsthwaite Chapel." (R.O. R.Taylor,jr)
Jan/Apr 1873: "Left his service."
27.06.1877:   "At his trade. No complaints."
24.03.1877:   "Apprenticeship expired"

EDMONDSON, Henry
Hired: 20.11.1866 (age 12)
Employer: James Housby, Tailor, North Scale, Walney.
Oct 1867:   "Quite satisfactory. Attends Walney Chapel and Sunday School regularly."
                (R.O. Geo. Simpson)
1870-1873:   William Ewart, Tailor, Paxton Street, Barrow.
                "No complaints. Attends Barrow Church." (R.O. R.Taylor)
02.01.1874:   "At his trade. Apprenticeship expired."

EDMONDSON, William
Hired: 27.07.1865 (age 12)
Employer: Abraham Slater, Blacksmith, North Scale.
Oct 1867:   "Quite satisfactory. Attends Walney Chapel." (R.O. R.Taylor,jr)
Oct 1872:   Apprenticeship expired.

FELL, James   b. Cartmel
Hired: 15.04.1874 (age 15)
Employer: Rushforth's Sunny Bank Bobbin Mill.
18.10.1876:   "Quite satisfied. Attends Torver Church." (R.O. Jas. Dickinson)
Oct 1877:   "Owing to Mr. Rushforth's death, this boy's apprenticeship expires, but he has made
                arrangements to stay with Mr. Rushforth's sons."
20.01.1879:   "Quite satisfied. Loose, but still works as a journeyman.(19)"
1871 Census: In workhouse – James D. Fell (10), no parent. *[G.Mins. Jly 1873: Report of ill treatment by schoolmaster. Sept 1873: 'Not fit for school, very nervous state']*

FELL, Robert   b. Ulverston
Hired: 13.05.1867 (age 11)
Employer: Michael J. Coupland, Sunny Bank Bobbin Mill, Torver.
Oct 1871:   "Master bankrupt. Indentures cancelled."
1861 Census: In workhouse (5) *[With mother, Mary Ann (31), U/M, b. Holker. Drawer in cotton mill, brother, Richard (7) and sister, Eliza (10months)]*
[See also William]

1862 Census: In workhouse. *[Orphan of William Dixon of Ulverston. Brother to William Dixon, below and sister, Mary Jane. Aunts in Preston]*

FELL, William   b. Ulverston
Hired: 14.10.1877 (age 14)
Employer: James Scott, Tailor, Ealingharth.
18.10.1878:   "Quite satisfied. Master expresses his satisfaction."
05.10.1879:   -do-
Jun 1881:   "Absconded"
1871 Census: In workhouse (8). *[With mother, Mary Ann (42), U/M, Cotton Spinner, b. Flookburgh, sister, Mary Ann (5), b. Ulverston and Margaret J. (1), b. Ulverston.] [William in Master's punishment book 1875/1876.]*
[N.B. Mother, Mary Ann shown in 1861 Census (31) with three older children – see Robert]

FORREST, George
Hired: 13.07.1865 (age 13)
Employer: Robert Hooker, Plumber & Glazier, Dalton and Barrow
Oct 1867:   "Quite satisfactory. Attends Barrow Chapel regularly."
1869:   "Ran away"

FORSYTH, James   from West Derby Union, Liverpool
Hired: May 1874 (age 14)
Employer: James Dixon, Hoopmaker, Sawrey.
                      "Attends Sawrey Church and School."
06.08.1874:   "Absconded, is at Barrow."
10.10.1876:   "Perfectly satisfactory. Master speaks highly of him." (R.O.)

FORSYTH, Joseph
Hired: 18.05.1874 (age 14)
Employer: James Dixon, Hoopmaker, Sawrey.
07.02.1875:   "Attends Sawrey Church"
10.10.1876:   "Perfectly satisfactory. Master speaks highly of him." *[James and Joseph were orphans. It is possible they were twins and that they were hired together, or it may be that their two records became mixed, as the Relieving Officer's comments are applied to both records. According to the Guardians' Minutes of October 1879, a Mr. John Taylor of Kendal was asked to take them, but said he was not in a position to support "the two orphans, Forsyth". In the following November, a place was offered for only one of the boys at a philanthropic institution under the management of Mr. Noble at Douglas, Isle of Man.]*

GELDART, Thomas
Hired: 02.07.1873 (age 13)
Employer: Isaac Creighton, Colton Bobbin Mill, Nibthwaite.
Aug 1876:   "Complained that Master struck him." (R.O. J. Nicholson)
Oct 1876:   "Does not like the trade. Complains of no clothes. Has 1 pair of stockings
                      bought them himself, had shirt on, only one besides."
Apr 1877:   Company became North Lonsdale Company.
Sep 1877:   "Absconded. Masters say he was employed at a turning machine and they
                      wanted him to go to a boring machine, but he refused and consequently left."
Jan 1878:   "At his trade. Quite satisfactory. Came back at Christmas."
Jly 1878:   "At his trade. Masters express their satisfaction." *[In Oct 1872 the Guardians agreed to send Thomas (12 yrs 6 months) to be apprentice in farm service with John Rawlinson of Cragg, Egton-with-Newland provided he had the 'usual' holidays and a suit of clothes on completion of service to the value of £5]*

GIBSON, Ann
Hired: 01.05.1872 (age 13)
Employer: Owen Wake, Foundry Man, 57 Preston Street, Barrow. (for Housework)
Jan 1873:   "Not satisfied. Attends Wesleyan Chapel." (R. Taylor, jr.)
Apr 1873:   "Left Barrow with her Master. Supposed gone to Hartlepool."
1871 Census: In workhouse. (11) *[With brother, Robert, see below.] [Aug. 1873 Ann Gibson, age 13, was sent as servant to Jas. Hamer, Ulverston @ 1s.6d. p.week. Same girl?]*

GIBSON, Robert   b. Cark
Hired: 17.06.1875 (age 15)
Employer: Henry Tyson, Farmer, Hobkinground, Broughton.
07.01.1876:   "Left service at Martinmas and came into the workhouse." (R.O. Jas Postlethwaite)
1871 Census: In workhouse [with sister, Ann (11)] *[Guardians' Minutes Dec 1872: Robert (age 11) was allowed to go to his uncle, John Gibson, of Crosthwaite Bobbin Mill. However, he must have returned to the workhouse as he was in the master's punishment book several times in 1875.]*

GIBSON, Thomas
Hired: 02.04.1874 (age -)
Employer: Thos. Whitwell, Blacksmith, Newton.
Oct 1874:   "Has absconded about Sept. 18th." (R.O. Jas. Swainson)
02.04.1875:   "At his trade. No complaints. Attends Newton Chapel."

Sep 1878:   "Left his Master."
Feb 1879:   "Not returned" *[G.Mins. 08.09.1879: Thomas had enlisted in the Army, 82nd Regiment.]*
[G.Mins. 04.06.1863: Thomas Gibson on trial at Force Forge (13) – possibly another boy.]

GIBSON, William
Hired: 28.04.1870 (age 14)
Employer: Robert Nelson, Tailor, Broughton West.
Jly 1870:   "No complaint. Broughton Church and Sunday School."(R.O. Jas Postlethwaite)
07.10.1870: "Had absconded"

GRAVES, Thomas
Hired: 14.04.1871 (age 13)
Employer: Moses Jackson, Tailor, Barrow.
15.04.1871: "Quite satisfied. Attends Wesleyan Chapel." (R.O. Geo. Simpson) *[Was he brother to Arthur and John? Spellings often varied.]*

GREAVES (Graves), Arthur   b. Ulverston
Hired: 26.09.1872 (age 12)
Employer: Isaac Myers, Tailor, Beckside, Kirkby Ireleth.
             "Attends St.Mary's Baptist Chapel and Sunday School" (R.O. Jas Postlethwaite)
Jan 1879:   "Finished Apprenticeship and worked for Master some time after."
1871 Census: In workhouse (10). [With brother, James (9)]. *[Arthur took over this position from his brother, John..*
In 1871 Census: James Greaves, Widr.(65), b. Ulverston - ? father]

GREAVES, James   b. Ulverston
Hired: 19.02.1874 (age 12)
Employer: Francis Postlethwaite, Tailor, Dalton.
11.04.1874: "Quite satisfied. Attends Dalton Church." (R.O. Geo. Simpson)
Jly 1874:   "No complaints."
1871 Census: In workhouse (9). *[Brother to Arthur and John]*

GREAVES, John
Hired: 29.11.1866 (age 12)
Employer: Isaac Myers, Tailor, Beckside, Kirkby Ireleth.
Oct 1867:   "Attends St. Mary's Baptist Chapel and Sunday School." (R.O. Jas Postlethwaite)
14.04.1871: "Quite satisfactory. Attends Baptist Chapel."
19.06.1871: Died, age 16, buried at Kirkby. *[Brother to Arthur, above.]*

GREGSON, Edward   from West Derby Union, Liverpool
Hired: 10.07.1872 (age 12)
Employer: Robinson's, Cunsey Bobbin Mill, Sawrey.
10.04.1877: "Found mill stopped. Boys peeling sticks in coppice wood."
04.10.1876: "Would like stockings for winter." *[05.08.1872: Guardians' minutes stated that Edward Gregson was only 10]*

GRIFFITHS, David   b. Scotland
Hired: 03.04.1873 (age 12)
Employer: Isaac Creighton, Colton Bobbin Mills, Nibthwaite.
Jly 1873:   "No complaints. Attends Blawith Chapel." (R.O. Roger Taylor)
17.10.1876: "Has no stockings."
09.01.1877: "Quite satisfied with food, treatment and clothing. Attends Blawith Church and
             Nibthwaite preaching room." (R.O. Jas Nicholson)
Apr 1877:   Became North Lonsdale & Co. Nibthwaite Mills.
1871 Census: In workhouse (10). *[With sister, Clara (7)[? died:22.03.1872] and brother, Gerald (2)]*

HADDAH, John
Hired: 29.04.1867 (age 14)
Employer: Geo. Baker, Basket Maker, Sykehouse, Backbarrow.
July 1867:   "Attends Baptist Chapel and Sunday School." (R.O. Jas Postlethwaite)
06.08.1867: "Absconded"
12.08.1867: Warrant Issued
Oct. 1868:   Still absent

HADWIN, Henry
Hired: 13.02.1872 (age 12)
Employer: Richard B. Creighton, Hooper, Backbarrow.
10.02.1873: "No complaints. Attends Backbarrow Chapel and Sunday School." (R.O. Jas. Swainson)

HARRIS, Henry   b. Ireland
Hired: 11.09.1873 (age 13)
Employer: John Walton, Tailor, Dalton.
Oct 1873:   "No complaints. Attends Dalton Church."
1871 Census: In workhouse (10). *[With brother John (6), b. Dalton]*

HARRISON, Benjamin
Hired: 10.08.1875 (age 11)
Employer: M. U H. Walker, Force Forge Bobbin Mill.
03.10.1876:   "Complained at having to bring his Mistress milk." (R.O. Jas Dickinson)
26.11.1878:   "Complained of having his stockings patched with fustian."
10.01.1879:   "Satisfied with clothes and work."

HARRISON, Edward
Hired: 08.10.1874 (age 13)
Employer: Wm. Blake, Shoemaker, 28 Forshaw Street, Barrow.
15.01.1875   "Satisfied. Attends Church." (R.O. R. Taylor)
09.07.1875:   "Very ill. Indentures cancelled by the Magistrates. Now in workhouse." *[Edward died 03.01.1876, aged 15, buried at Holy Trinity Church, Ulverston.]*

HEYWOOD, John   from West Derby Union, Liverpool.
Hired: 07.01.1874 (age 13)
Employer: John Airey, Farmer, Cunsey Farm, Sawrey.
Mar. 1874:   "Attends Sawrey Church" (R.O. Jas Dickinson)
24.07.1879:   "Quite satisfactory. Now receives wages."

HOLMES, Elizabeth
Hired: 14.07.1870 (age 13)
Employer: Daniel Braithwaite, Cordwainer, Hindpool, Barrow. (for Housework)
Oct 1871:   "Has left her situation and hired herself elsewhere." (R.O. Geo Simpson)

HOLMES, Jane
Hired: August 1872 (age 12)
Employer: Wm. Spencer, Grocer, 60 Ramsden Street, Barrow. (for Housework)
Jan 1873:   "Quite satisfied. Attends Wesleyan Chapel." (R.O. R. Taylor, jr.)
15.01.1875:   "Left her service and re-hired." *[Guardians' Mins: Aug 1872 sent to work for Mr. Brignall of Barrow, but found not satisfactory and returned, then sent to Mr.Spencer]*

HORNBY, Elizabeth
Hired: 01.11.1869 (age 13)
Employer: Charles Stewart, Glass & China Dealer, Queen St., Ulverston. (for Housework)
July 1870:   "No complaints. Attends new and old Church" (R.O. Jas Riley)

HORNBY, Jane   b. Ireleth
Hired: 01.10.1872 (age12) (actually 11)
Employer: Richard Bell, Draper, Ireleth Marsh. (for Housework)
                (Harris Street, Barrow)
03.10.1872:   Approved by Board of Guardians at 1s6d per week
1871 Census: In workhouse, age 10 *[with mother, Ann (41) married, Domestic Servant b. Urswick Sarah (12) b. Ireleth, Robert (8) b Ireleth.]*
[A Robert Hornby of 13 Bigg Rigg Moor, Egremont is mentioned in the Guardians' Minutes of 1868 as having wife and children at Kirkby Ireleth. Perhaps being sought for their support.]

HUGHES, Frances
Hired: 10.01.1867 (age -)
Employer: Henry Rawsthorne, Farmer, Birkby. (for Housework)
Oct 1867:   "No complaints. Attends Cartmel Chapel." (R.O. Roger Taylor, jr)
10.01.1868:   "Term of hiring expired. Came into house."

HUGHES, John Benjamin   from West Derby Union, Liverpool
Hired: 10.07.1872 (age 14)
Employer: Jos. Robinson, Cunsey Bobbin Mill, Sawrey.
10.04.1877:   "Found the mill stopped and was told by Mrs. Robinson that the boys were peeling sticks in a coppice wood at some distance." (R.O. Jas Dickinson)

HUGHES, Thomas   from West Derby Union, Liverpool
Hired: 10.07.1872 (age 13)
Employer: Jos. Robinson, Cunsey Bobbin Mill, Sawrey.
04.10.1876:   "Stated he would like stockings for winter. Asked for shoe rings for winter." (R.O. Jas Dickinson)
10.04.1877:   "Found the mill stopped…"
Jan 1879:   "This boy completed his apprenticeship and now works as a journeyman with Mr. Robinson."

HUGHES, William   from West Derby Union, Liverpool
Hired: 10.07.1872 (age 11)
Employer: Cunsey Bobbin Mill, Sawrey.
Aug 1873:   "Attends Sawrey Church and half-time school." (R.O. Jas Dickinson)
16.08.1874:   Absconded

04.10.1876:   At Cunsey. "Would like stockings for winter."
10.04.1877:   "Found the mill stopped…" *[Guardians' Minutes 05.08.1872: William was one of the boys sent from West Derby to work at Cunsey described by the Guardians as 'too young…work too hard' and his age given as 10 yrs]*

JACKSON, Mary Jane   from Liverpool
Hired: 10.03.1872 (age 13)
Employer: Jas. F. Blacklock, Toy Shop, Market Street, Ulverston. (for Housework)
27.06.1873:   "Has left to go back to mother at Liverpool"

JOHNSON, William
Hired: 06.07.1877 (age 15)
Employer: Rushforth's Sunny Bank Bobbin Mill, Torver.
12.02.1879:   "Bobbin Mill burned down – Removed to Cockermouth"

KEITH, Margaret   b. Dudley, Staffs.
Hired: 03.10.1872 (age 12)
Employer: Wm. Bell, Sowerby Lodge. (for Housework)
Jly 1873:   "No complaints. Attends Newbarns Church." (R.Taylor, jr.)
1871 Census: In workhouse. *[With mother, Margaret (40), married, dom.serv., b. Dudley, Staffs., sisters, Maria (12), Eliza(8), and brothers, Michael (7), John(3).All born in Dudley except John, b. Barrow.]*

KEITH, Maria   b. Dudley, Staffs.
Hired: 08.07.1871 (age 13)
Employer: Thos. Mashiter, Woollen Draper, Neville Street, Ulverston. (for Housework)
09.10.1871:   "No complaints. Attends Catholic Chapel." (R.O. Jas. Riley)
Jun 1872:   "Has left her place and been engaged to Windermere." *[Sister to Margaret, above.]*

KELLETT, James
Hired: 31.01.1862 (age 11)
Employer: Wm. Casson Holmes, Tailor, Beckside, Kirkby Ireleth.
July 1867:   "No complaints. Attends Kirkby Church." (R.O. Jas. Postlethwaite)
Jan 1869:   Finished Apprenticeship.
1861 Census: In workhouse. *[With mother, Mary (36), U/M, Farm Servant, b. Colton, sister, Elizabeth (6)]*

KERRY, James   from Stratford-upon-Avon
Hired: 10.05.1875 (age 13)
Employer: Force Forge Bobbin Mill, Satterthwaite.
04.04.1877:   "Complained of having to wear ragged clothes." (R.O. Jas Dickinson)
July 1878:   "No water to run the mill."

KING, Elizabeth
Hired: (age 13)
Employer: Jas. Harrison, Joiner, Dalton Road, Barrow. (for Housework)
July 18790:   "Had left her service and left the place." (R.O. Geo. Simpson)

KING, Thomas Graves
Hired: 14.04.1870 (age 13)
Employer: Moses Jackson, Tailor, Hindpool Road, Barrow.
July 1870:   "Quite satisfactory. Attends Barrow Church." (R.O. Geo. Simpson)

LATIMER, Thomas   b. Carlisle
Hired: 07.11.1872
Employer: Nicholas Mandell, Plumber & Painter, Ireleth Marsh and Stafford Street, Askam.
Jan 1873:   "Quite satisfactory. Attends Ireleth Chapel."
Apr 1873:   Indentures had been cancelled
Hired: 22.05.1873 (age 14)
Employer: M & H Walker, Force Forge Bobbin Mill, Satterthwaite.
30.05.1875:   "Complains Master opens his letters and keeps them" (R.O. Jas Dickinson)
03.10.1876:   "Complained of having to saw all his time and not doing other work."
1876 and 1877:-do- also "Complained about scarcity of food."
02.01.1877:   -do- "but the boy having returned from his holidays at the time fixed, the Master
                promised not to do it any more. With this promise, he was satisfied."
31.07.1878:   "Complains of not having suitable clothing."
10.01.1879:   "Left by consent of masters." Appeared before the Guardians and the Indentures ordered to be cancelled.
1871 Census: In workhouse (12), no parent shown.

LITHGOW, James
Hired: 10.07.1872 (age 13)
Employer: Cunsey Bobbin Mill, Sawrey.
25.11.1873:   "Ran away" (R.O. Jas Dickinson)
March 1874:   Away
July 1874:   Back at work.

43

LOCKLEY, William   from Liverpool
Hired: 13.02.1873 (age 13)
Employer: E. & W. Coward, Stott Park Bobbin Mill, Finsthwaite.
April 1873:   "No complaints. Attends Finsthwaite Chapel."
12.07.1878:   "Complaints of food. Master complains of his conduct."
04.10.1878:   "Quite satisfactory."
1881 Census: Listed as bobbin turner at Stott Park.

MACKERETH, John   b. Holker Lower
Hired: 09.04.1863 (age 14)
Employer: Jas. Kirkby Richardson, Cordwainer, North Scale.
Oct 1867:   "Attends Walney Chapel regularly." (R.O. Geo. Simpson)
Jan 1870:   "No complaints. Out of apprenticeship (18 yrs.)."
1861 Census: In workhouse *[With brother, George (9), no parent shown.]*
Nov 1862:   Uncle, Thomas Rose of Flookburgh took him and brother, George, out of
                workhouse for one week. *[If John was 18 in Jan 1870, he must only have been 11 yrs. old when hired. This may have been a mistake as the Guardians' Minutes state him to be 14 yrs. old on 10.01.1863 before being Indentured.]*

MACKERETH, George   b. Holker Lower
Hired: 07.07.1865 (age 13)
Employer: Francis Withers Kendall, Cordwainer, Hindpool, Barrow.
Oct 1867:   "Quite satisfactory. Attends Barrow Church regularly." (R.O. Geo. Simpson)
Jan 1869:   "Ran away"
July 1869:   "Returned"
07.07.1871:   "At his trade – he is now loose of his apprenticeship."
1861 Census: In workhouse. *[With brother, John, above. No parent shown.]*

MANSELL, William   from Newcastle-under-Lyme
Hired: 03.10.1872 (age 13)
Employer: Jos. Taylor, Bobbin Turner and Brushmaker, Broughton.
Jan 1873:   "No complaints. Attends Church and Sunday School." (R.O. Jas. Postlethwaite)
May 1873:   "Firm left district. Gone to Ulverston."
26.04.1873   "At Low Mill, Ulverston. Attends Church."
Oct 1877:   "At Low Mill."
1871 Census: In workhouse (13).
[G. Mins. Aug 1872: Left Mr. Slater, Ambleside. Indentures transferred to Jos. Taylor]

MARTIN, James   b. Dalton
Hired: 02.05.1872 (age 12)
Employer: Joseph Taylor, Bobbin Turner & Brushmaker, Broughton.
Jan 1873:   "No complaints. Attends Church and Sunday School." (R.O. Jas Postlethwaite)
Jly 1873:   "Firm moved to Low Mill, Ulverston."
1871 Census: In workhouse (10). *[With sister, Agnes (8), b. Ireleth. Orphans of James and Mary Martin]*
[James's was Indentured on 05.09.1872 – including a clause giving 5s. per annum pocket money for first four years and 10s. p.a. for remainder. Agnes sent to Howard Home 08.07.1872 age 10. She died in Kendal on 06.05.1883]

MASHITER, John
Hired: 18.05.1865 (age 15)
Employer: John Fleming, Blacksmith, Newby Bridge.
Oct 1867-
Jan 1868:   "No complaints. Attends Staveley Chapel." (R.O. Roger Taylor, jr)
Jan 1871:   "Apprenticeship expired." *[Guardians' Minutes of 16.10.1862 show a Richard Mashiter in an Asylum in Faversham and his three children in a workhouse there. As their settlement was Ulverston, is John one of these three, transferred to Ulverston workhouse? See Edward, below.]*

MASHITER, Edward
Hired: 13.07.1865 (age 12)
Employer: E. & W. Coward, Stott Park Bobbin Mill.
Oct 1867:   "No complaints. Attends Finsthwaite Chapel." (R.O. Roger Taylor, jr)
Oct 1872:   "At his trade. Apprenticeship expired." *[Brother of John, above.]*

MASON, James   b. Ulverston
Hired: 09.11.1865 (age 12)
Employer: Walker's, Force Forge Bobbin Mill, Satterthwaite.
Nov. 1867:   "No complaints. Attends Satterthwaite Chapel."
06.10.1871   "Apprenticeship expired."
Mar 1873:   "Out of his time. At his trade as Journeyman.."
1861 Census: In workhouse (6). *[With father, George (52) Widower, Ag.Lab., b.Heversham and brother, Robert (9) b. Egton (see below)]*

MASON, Robert   b. Egton
(Not in R.Os' Register – Ref: Guardians' Minutes – See added list)
[Brother to James above]

44

McMILLAN, Hugh   from West Derby Union, Liverpool.
Hired: 06.08.1874 (age 13)
Employer: William Bolton, Painter, Hawkshead.
10.10.1876:   "Perfectly satisfactory. Attends Hawkshead Church."
30.06.1879:   "Doing well. Employed as Painter & Glazier."

MILLER, Thomas
Hired: ? 1877
Employer: Jackson Coward, Skelwith Bridge Bobbin Mill.
08.08.1877:   "Quite satisfied. Attends Brathey Church." (age 19)
22.08.1878:   "Out of his time." (age 21)

O'NEIL, Daniel   from West Derby Union, Liverpool
Hired: 01.07.1867 (age 14)
Employer: Jos. Robinson, Cunsey Bobbin Mill, Sawrey.
22.05.1868:   "Complains of ill usage" (R.O. Jas Swainson)
July 1870:   "Had left"
July 1874:   "Returned"
10.01.1876:   "Returned to West Derby Union Workhouse on account of ill health."

OWENS, Thomas   from West Derby Union, Liverpool.
Hired: 11.02.1869 (age 13)
Employer: E. & W. Coward, Stott Park Bobbin Mill, Finsthwaite.
Apr 1869:   "Satisfactory. Attends Finsthwaite Chapel." (R.O. Roger Taylor, jr)
Jly 1870:   "Had left"
Jly 1872:   "Run away"
Jan 1873:   "At his trade"
25.03.1873   "Absconded"
July 1874:   "Returned"
Jan 1876:   "Returned to West Derby Union Workhouse on account of ill health."

PAINTER, George   from Liverpool
Hired: 04.04.1875 (age 15)
Employer: W. & J. Coward, Stott Park Bobbin Mill.
1881 Census: Shown at Stott Park Mill, age 20. *[Related to William?]*

PAINTER, William   from Liverpool
Hired: 08.08.1872 (age 14)
Employer: E. & W. Coward, Stott Park Bobbin Mill, Finsthwaite.
Jun 1873:   "No complaints. Attends Finsthwaite Chapel."
Apr 1878:   "Quite satisfactory"
Jly 1878:   (W. & J. Coward) "Complains about food. Masters not satisfied by his conduct."
Aug 1878:   "Apprenticeship expired." *[Related to George?]*

PARK, John
Hired: 21.04.1874 (age 13)
Employer: M. & H. Walker, Force Forge Bobbin Mill.
U/D Visit: "Quite satisfied. Attends Satterthwaite Church." (R.O. Jas. Dickinson) *[A John Park was in the Master's punishment book*
15.01.1876, age 15. Was this same boy?]

PENNEY, Mary
Hired: 25.03.1871 (age 12)
Employer: Mr. Shawcross, Farmer, Lane House. (for Housework)
07.10.1871:   "No complaints. Attends New Church." (R.O. Jas. Riley)
Jan 1873:   "Has hired herself to Burton-in-Lonsdale. *[Was she sister to John (below)?]*

PENNY, John   b. Bouth
Hired: 03.04.1873 (age 14)
Employer: Isaac Creighton, Colton Bobbin Mill, Nibthwaite.
17.10.1876:   "Complained, only one pair of stockings."
1877:   Mill became owned by North Lonsdale Co.
09.01.1877:   "Quite satisfactory."
18.04.1877:   "Unable to attend Church having no Sunday shoes, but his Masters have promised
              a pair of new ones."
1871 Census: In workhouse (age 9). *[With mother, Elizabeth, (41), Widow, Dom.Serv., b. St.Austell,*
Cornwall, brother, Rowley (7) b.Bouth, sister, Elizabeth (3) b. Bouth and Margaret (2) b. in the workhouse.]

PHIZACKLEA, Henry   from Liverpool
Hired: 08.08.1872 (age 14)
Employer: E. & W. Coward, Stott Park Bobbin Mill.
Jun 1873:   "No complaints."

12.07.1878:   (W. & J. Coward) "Complains about food – Masters not satisfied by his conduct."
Aug 1878:   "Apprenticeship expired."

PURDY, John   ? West Derby Union
Hired: 01.07.1867 (age 15)
Employer: Jos. Robinson, Cunsey Bobbin Mill, Sawrey.
22.05.1868:   "Complains of ill usage." (R.O. Jas Swainson)
Aug 1873:   "Out of his time. At his trade."

RICHARDS, Richard James
Hired: 23.07.1868 (age 11)
Employer: Wm. Casson, Blacksmith, Dalton.
Oct 1868:   "No complaint. Attends Dalton Church." (R.O. Geo. Simpson)

RIGG, James   b. Allithwaite Upper
Hired: 11.06.1863 (age 13)
Employer: Casson Barr, Boot & Shoe Maker, Beckside, Kirkby Ireleth.
Oct 1867:   "Attends St. Mary's Baptist Chapel and Sunday School."
1861 Census: In workhouse (11). *[With mother, Sarah (43) married, b. Allithwaite, brother, Henry (13), sisters, Margaret (7) and Sarah (4), all b. Allithwaite.]*
[G's Mins: Robert Kirkby of Ulpha also applied for James, but G's preferred Barr as he was in the Union.]

RIMMER, Martha Jane
Hired: 17.01.1874 (age -)
Employer: Jos. Robinson, Cunsey Bobbin Mill.
Mar 1874:   "At her work. Quite satisfied. Attends Sawrey Church." (R.O. Jas Dickinson)

ROBINSON, John
Hired: 13.05.1867 (age 12)
Employer: Michael Coupland, Sunny Bank Bobbin Mill, Torver.
Oct 1871:   "Master bankrupt. Indentures cancelled."

ROBINSON, Margaret
Hired: 13.01.1871 (age 13)
Employer: Wm. Heslam, (Clerk of the Canal Office), Canal Side, Ulverston. (for Housework)
1871:   "No complaints. Attends Wesleyan Chapel."
Oct 1871:   "Mistress not satisfied."
Hired: 01.01.1872 (age 14)
Employer: Isaac Sellers Berry, Shoemaker, Market Street, Ulverston.
06.01.1874:   "This young person is now emancipated." (Still at work) *[Mary Ann Robinson died in the workhouse on 15.05.1858, was this Margaret's mother?]*

ROBINSON, Thomas   b. Cartmel
Hired: 25.04.1872 (age 12)
Employer: John Walton, Tailor, Dalton.
Jly 1872:   "No complaints. Attends Dalton Church" (R.O. Geo. Simpson)
1871 Census: In workhouse (11), no parent shown. *[With sister, Margaret (7), b. Cartmel. Margaret went to the Howard Home at Kendal on 16.01.1873]*

ROBSON, Thomas
Hired: ? 1878 (age 13)
Employer: Henry Nelson, Tailor, The Ellers, Ulverston.
03.01.1879:   "No complaints. Attends to the Congregational Church and Sabbath School." (R.O. Jas. Riley)

ROMNEY, Margaret   b. Dalton
Hired: 11.04.1872 (age 12)
Employer: Anna Bilsborough, Grocer, 124 Cavendish Street, Barrow. (for Housework)
Jan 1873:   "Quite satisfied. Attends Wesleyan Chapel." (R.O. R.Taylor, jr.)
Jly 1873:   "Left her service"
1871 Census: In workhouse, no parent shown *[With brother, Samuel R. (10)]*

SANTER, Mary Jane
Hired: 14.11.1868 (age 15)
Employer: Elizabeth Ormandy, Farmer, Lindale Coat. (for Housework)
Feb 1869:   "Quite satisfactory. Attends Lindale Chapel regularly." (R.O. Geo. Simpson)
Oct 1869:   "Left her situation and hired elsewhere."

SHARP, William
Hired: 14.12.1870 (age 14)
Employer: Thos. Shuttleworth, Cordwainer, Dalton.
Oct 1871:   "No complaint. Attends Dalton Church regularly."
Apr 1873:   "Left his place and gone away. Not known where."

SHAW, Croasdale
Hired: 02.02.1871 (age 15)
Employer: Michael J. Coupland, Sunny Bank Bobbin Mill, Torver.
Oct 1871:   "Master bankrupt. Indentures cancelled."

SHEARSON, Richard   from West Derby Union.
Hired: 10.07.1872 (age 11)
Employer: Jos. Robinson, Cunsey Bobbin Mill, Sawrey.
Aug 1873:   "Quite satisfied. Attends Sawrey Church and half-time school." (R.O. Jas. Dickinson) *[Richard was one of the boys the*
Guardians had thought too young and the work too hard. G.Mins.05.08.1872]

SMITH, Alice
Hired: 01.05.1868 (age 11)
Employer: Jos. Robinson, Cunsey Bobbin Mill, Sawrey.
22.05.1868: "Complains of ill usage. At his trade." (R.O. Jas Swainson)
Nov. 1868:   "No complaints."
July 1869:   "Had left service."

SMITH, John
Hired: 16.08.1878 (age 15)
Employer: William Crellin, Farmer, Moss Cottage, Broughton.
28.03.1879: "Quite satisfied. Attends Broughton Church and Sunday School." (R.O. Jas. Postlethwaite)

SMITH, John Postlethwaite   b. Dalton
Hired: 1864 (age 12)
Employer: Isaac Hadwin, Tailor, of Grange.
10.01.1867: Indentures cancelled.
Hired: 14.02.1867 (age 14)
Employer: Walker's, Force Forge Bobbin Mill.
Nov. 1867:   "No complaints. Attends Satterthwaite Chapel."
1861 Census: In workhouse (9). *[With mother, Elizabeth(37), married b. Dalton, brother, Robert (7)*
b. Hensingham and sister, Isabella (1), b. Hensingham.]

THACKERAY, Elizabeth
Hired: 1874 (age 13)
Employer: Thomas Graves, Steel Works' Labourer, Barrow. (for Housework)
10.04.1874: "No complaints." (R.O. R.Taylor)
Jly 1874:   "Left her situation 5 weeks ago."
19.04.1875: "At John Street, Barrow. Housework. No complaints."
Jly 1875:   "Left her service with the consent of her employer and re-hired."

THACKERAY, William
Hired: 20.02.1870 (age 14)
Employer: Wm. Gaskell, Tanner, High Nibthwaite.
Aug 1874:   "Quite satisfied. Attends Blawith Church." (R.O. Jno Nicholson)
24.02.1877: "Apprenticeship expired."

TOOMEY, Michael
Hired: 09.11.1865 (age 13)
Employer: Walker's, Force Forge Bobbin Mill.
Nov 1867:   "No complaints. Attends Satterthwaite Chapel." (R.O. Jas Swainson)
Oct 1868:   "Absconded"

TODD, Christopher
Hired: 02.07.1874 (age 13)
Employer: Richard Harding, Tailor, Union Street, Ulverston.
U/D Visit: "Attends Independent Chapel (Congregational)."

TOWNSON, John
Hired: 26.01.1871 (age 12)
Employer: Hugh H. Towers, Force Forge Bobbin Mill.
Oct 1871:   "Quite satisfied. Attends Rusland Church." (R.Os. Jas. Swainson/Jas. Dickinson)

TURNER, Edward
Hired: 27.02.1873 (age 13)
Employer: Thos. Melish, Shoemaker, Dalton.
Jly 1873:   "No complaints. Attends Wesleyan Chapel." (R.O. Geo. Simpson)

TYSON, John
Hired: 12.04.1866 (age 12)
Employer: Michael Rawlinson, Tailor, Scales.
Sep 1867:   "Quite satisfactory. Attends Aldingham Church." (R.O. Geo. Simpson)
Oct 1871:   "He is now loose of his apprenticeship. His master is dead and he has re-bound himself."
Jan 1872:   "At his trade. Quite satisfied."

TYSON, Robert
Hired: 20.10.1870 (age 13)
Employer: M. & H. Walker, Force Forge Bobbin Mill.
Oct 1871:   "Quite satisfied. Attends Satterthwaite Chapel." (R.O. Jas. Swainson)
20.10.1877:   "Completed his apprenticeship (19). Went to work at Clapham." (R.O. Jas. Dickinson)

WALKER, Edward
Hired: 10.08.1875 (age 11)
Employer: Stott Park Bobbin Mill.
10.06.1876:   "Complained about having no stockings." (Jas. Dickinson)
03.10.1876:   "Returned to the workhouse
Hired: 20.10.1876 (age 12)
Employer: John Mathers, Clogger & Shoemaker, Coniston.
05.01.1877:   "Likes his work. Attends day school half time."
23.06.1879:   "Master speaks very well of him."
23.11.1881:   "Doing very well."

WATSON, Thomas   from West Derby Union, Liverpool.
Hired: 06.08.1874 (age 13)
Employer: James Postlethwaite, Tailor and Innkeeper, Hawkshead.
10.10.1876:   "Perfectly satisfied. Attends Hawkshead Church."
July 1877:   "Deserted, but back to parents."
07.07.1877:   "At his trade. This boy is now out of the care of the Guardians. Was deserted but now owned by parents." (Jas Dickinson)

WHALLEY, John
Hired: 06.07.1877 (age 11)
Employer: Rushforth's Sunny Bank Bobbin Mill.
12.02.1879:   "Bobbin Mill burned down. Removed to Cockermouth."

WHITE, Hannah
Hired: 25.10.1867 (age 14)
Employer: W.H.Mellor, Tea Dealer, Morecambe Road, Ulverston. (for Housework)
1867:   "Master and mistress not satisfied with her. She promises amendment. Attends New Church Chapel." (R.O. Jas. Riley)
Mar 1868:   "No complaint. Attending child."
July 1868:   "Hired herself to John Murthwaite, Grocer."
1861 Census: In workhouse (8), no parent. *[Son, George Arthur, born in workhouse 14.10.1871]*

WHITFIELD, Samuel
Hired: 01.07.1867 (age 15)
Employer: Jos. Robinson, Cunsey Bobbin Mill, Sawrey.
22.05.1868:   "Complains of ill usage." (R.O. Jas Swainson)
Aug 1873:   "Out of his time. Working as Journeyman Bobbin Turner. Attends Sawrey Church."

WILKINSON, William Thomas   b. Ulverston
Hired: 16.11.1865 (age 15)
Employer: Michael Rawlinson, Tailor, Scales.
Sep 1867:   "Quite satisfied. Attends Aldingham Church."
Oct 1871:   "At his trade. Now out of apprenticeship."
1861 Census: In workhouse (10), no parent shown. *[With sister, Eleanor (6), b. Ulverston.]*

WILLIAMSON, Robert
Hired: 29.01.1863 (age 11)   b. Southport
Employer: Thomas Preston, Tailor, Dalton.
Oct 1867:   "Neither Master nor boy quite satisfied."
Jan 1868:   "Not quite satisfied."
Oct 1868:   "No complaint. Attends Dalton Church."
Apr 1869:   "Church not very regular."
1861 Census: In workhouse (9), no parent shown. *[With sister, Hannah (12), b. Southport]*
[Robert's apprenticeship was at first deferred because he was being treated for skin disease. – G.Mins.]

WILSON, John
Hired: 08.11.1873 (age 12)
Employer: Rev. Charles Mortlock, Vicar, Pennington Vicarage.
20.07.1874:   "Housework. No complaints. Attends Pennington Church." (Jas. Riley)
03.04.1875:   "Removed to Barrow, with consent of the Board."
[In G.Mins. 28.08.1873, John (11yr.10m) was considered for apprenticeship with Abraham Barker, Basket maker, Broughton, but it was declined because he was too young.]

Many entries in the Register contain discrepancies in names, ages, etc., and have been corrected when further information came to light. The Relieving Officers were keen to show church attendance because this was usually a condition of apprenticeship. The children were supposed to have Sunday free for learning, after Church, but, in the mills, it is suspected they were often made to clean machinery, etc, whilst the mill was quiet.. Towards the end of the register the records became very sketchy and were not diligently kept.

The following records have been taken from Guardians' Minute books, where details were brief.

09.02.1837	Before new workhouse opened.
AKISTER, Aaron (8).	Apprenticed to Mr. Spencer, Shoemaker (and suit of clothes).
30.10.1862:	
FELL, Elizabeth	Not agreed to allow her to go to Thos. Hartley of Bardsea, Labourer,as a servant at 9d. per week for six months.
POOL, Mary Eleanor (12)	As a servant for six months at wage of 9d. per week to Joseph Postlethwaite, King Street, Ulverston. The Board allowing the usual clothing. Agreed.
06.11.1862:	
IRELAND, Thomas	Hired to John Barker of Lindend, Broughton West, on 6 May 1862 until Whitsuntide at 1s. per week. Agreed.
13.11.1862:	
THOMPSON, Eleanor	(Returned from Service).
	To go to James Storey of Greenbank, Cartmel, Farmer, as servant until next Whitsuntide at 1s.3d. per week if Board allowed 3s.10d. for additional clothing. 18.12.1862: Said girl did not give satisfaction, asked for Ann Brockbank instead. Agreed. 24.12.1862: Retained Thompson, sent Brockbank back.
05.02.1863:	
BROCKBANK, Ann (15)	To Mr. Peter Redhead of Sunderland Terrace, Ulverston, as servant until Whitsuntide at 9d. per week.
12.02.1863:	
MASON, Robert	Apprenticed to John Parker, Soutergate, Kirkby Ireleth.(age 11). 1863: Absconded. Guardians requested Mr. Cooper,. Superintendent of Police to make enquiries 19.03.1863: John Parker ordered to have boy apprehended.
	1861 Census: In workhouse (9) b. Egton - with Father, George (52), widower, Ag.Lab., b. Heversham and brother James (6) See main list.
TOWERS, Mary	Hired to James Eddy, Dalton – left her place.
TOWERS, Thomas	With Thomas Tyson of Ulverston – is idle and disobedient.
07.05.1863:	
KELLETT, John	Apprenticed aboard Schooner "Mary Anne" (owners, Jas. Fisher, Barrow) –Absconded.
August 1872:	
PURDEY, William (10)	From West Derby Union. To Jos. Robinson, Cunsey Bobbin Mill.
EDMONDSON ? (10)	From West Derby Union. To Jos. Robinson, Cunsey Bobbin Mill.
ANDREWS, Joel (13)	From Salford Union. To Coward's, Stott Park Mill.
SHAW, William (13)	From Salford Union. to Coward's, Stott Park Mill.
	1891 Census: At Stott Park age 22. b. Kirkdale.

(Ulverston Guardians suggested these boys be paid 5s per annum pocket money for first four years and 10s. p.a. for remainder. Bound for 7 years.)

HADWEN, Leonard ⎤	Orphans. Living with, or hired to:
HADWEN, Richard ⎦	Matthew Slater, Row Redding, Nr. Ulverston.
SMETHURST, James	From Fylde Union: Bound to Thomas Ward, Clogger, Ulverston.
GREGSON, James	From Fylde Union: Bound to John Bayliff, Currier, Dragley Beck, Ulverston.
ROSSALL, Robert	From Fylde Union: Bound to George Wilson, Tanner, Colton.

BIBLIOGRAPHY

Neil Tonge: "Industrialisation & Society 1700-1914"
(Thos. Nelson & Sons Ltd. 1993)

M.A.Crowther: "The Workhouse System 1834-1929"
(Batsford Ltd. 1981)

Simon Schama: "The History of Britain" Vol.3
(BBC Worldwide Ltd., London. 2002)

Peter Aughton: "Liverpool: A People's History"
(Carnegie Publishing Ltd., Preston. 1990)

June Rose: "For the Sake of the Children – Inside Dr. Barnardo's"
(Hodder & Staughton, London. 1987)

J.D.Marshall: "Furness and the Industrial Revolution 1711-1900"
(Barrow-in-Furness Library & Museum Committee 1958)

Derek Whale: "Lost Villages of Liverpool Part 3"
(T. Stephenson & Sons Ltd., Prescot, Merseyside. 1984)

Jeannie Duckworth: "Fagin's Children: Criminal Children in Victorian
England". (Hambledon and London, London. 2002)

Frank Crompton: "Workhouse Children"
(Sutton Publishing Ltd., Stroud, Glos. 1997)

John Marsh. "The Lake Counties at Work"
(Alan Sutton Publishing Ltd., Stroud, Glos. 1995)

J.D.Marshall and John K.Walton: "The Lake Counties 1830-mid Twentieth
Century" (Manchester University Press 1981)

Michael Rose: "The English Poor Law 1780-1930"
(David & Charles, Newton Abbot. 1971)

Peter White BA FSA: "Guide Book to Stott Park Bobbin Mill"
(English Heritage Publication)

"Kirkby Ireleth Select Vestry Book 1819-1908"
(Transcription Published by 'History of Kirkby Group' 2005)
Copy in Barrow-in-Furness Record Office

CUMBRIA RECORD OFFICE & LOCAL STUDIES LIBRARY,
BARROW-IN-FURNESS:-

Census Returns 1851: HO/107/2274 – Backbarrow Folio 216/210 and
Sparkbridge Folio 358)
Census Returns for Ulverston Workhouse: 1841 to 1901
Extracts from: "Soulby's Ulverston Advertiser": 6th and 20th June 1878
and 18th July 1878
Holy Trinity Church Register, Ulverston and Ulverston Cemetery Records
St. Cuthbert's Church Kirkby Ireleth Parish Records

ULVERSTON POOR LAW UNION (C.R.O. Barrow Ref: BT/HOS/UU)
1/3   Letter Book (In) from Poor Law Commissioners
2/4   Standing Order Book 1836-1843
2/6   Apprenticeship Indenture: William Threlfall
2/7   Register of Visits by Relieving Officer to Young Persons Under 16
         1863-1879
2/8   Apprenticeship Indenture: John Postlethwaite Smith
2/9   Register of Deaths in Workhouse 1866-1916
2/10   Register of Births in Workhouse 1866-1948
2/11/1   Register of Punishments 1874-1954
         Master's Inventory Book (Undated)
3/3   Visiting Committee's Report Book 1887-1893
3/4   Master's Report Book 1891-1893
3/5   Visiting Committee's Report Book 1895-1898

50

ULVERSTON POOR LAW UNION (Ref: PUU/)
8/9   Letter Books (In) from Local Government Board 02/01/1878-16/12/1878
10/7   Letter Books In and Out: 01/01/1898-23/12/1898
10/8   Letter Books In and Out: 01/01/1899-26/12/1900

ULVERSTON POOR LAW UNION: (Ref: PUU/1/)
GUARDIANS' MINUTE BOOKS:
/1   26/08/1836-18/10/1838
/2   25/10/1838-10/03/1841
/9   18/09/1862-08/02/1866
/10   15/02/1866-05/08/1869
/11   12/08/1869-23/05/1872
/12   30/05/1872-15/04/1875
/14   18/04/1878-15/09/1881
/15   29/09/1881-26/03/1885
/18   02/04/1891-28/03/1894
/20   16/07/1896-19/01/1899
/21   02/02/1899-07/11/1901

FURNESS COLLECTION (C.R.O. Barrow-in-Furness):
Z.1674   Ulverston Workhouse Rules (POOR LAW COMMISSION Regulations 1838)
Z.1023/3   Plans of Children's Quarters – December 1897

CUMBRIA C. C. RECORD OFFICE (KENDAL)
Westmorland Orphans' Home: List of Inmates 1865-1888
and Howard Home Register (Ref. WD/MM Box 181)

LIVERPOOL RECORD OFFICE
Kirkdale Industrial Schools Classification Registers:
October 1871-March 1880 (Ref. 353 SEL)

www.workhouses.org.uk